MATHEMATICIANS
AND STATISTICIANS

PRACTICAL CAREER GUIDES

Series Editor: Kezia Endsley

MATHEMATICIANS AND STATISTICIANS

A Practical Career Guide

KEZIA ENDSLEY

ROWMAN & LITTLEFIELD

Lanham • Boulder • New York • London

Published by Rowman & Littlefield
An imprint of The Rowman & Littlefield Publishing Group, Inc.
4501 Forbes Boulevard, Suite 200, Lanham, Maryland 20706
www.rowman.com

6 Tinworth Street, London, SE11 5AL, United Kingdom

British Library Cataloguing in Publication Information Available

Library of Congress Cataloging-in-Publication Data

Names: Endsley, Kezia, 1968– author.
Title: Mathematicians and statisticians : a practical career guide / Kezia
  Endsley.
Description: Lanham : Rowman & Littlefield, [2021] | Series: Practical
  career guides | Includes bibliographical references. | Summary:
  "Mathematicians and Statisticians: A Practical Career Guide includes
  interviews with professionals in a field that has proven to be a stable,
  lucrative, and growing profession. If you're looking for a career as a
  statistician, college math professor, actuary, research analyst or
  economist this is the book for you"—Provided by publisher.
Identifiers: LCCN 2020052295 (print) | LCCN 2020052296 (ebook) | ISBN
  9781538145166 (cloth) | ISBN 9781538145173 (ebook)
Subjects: LCSH: Mathematics—Vocational guidance. | Mathematicians. |
  Statistics—Vocational guidance. | Statisticians.
Classification: LCC QA10.5 .E53 2021 (print) | LCC QA10.5 (ebook) | DDC
  510.23—dc23
LC record available at https://lccn.loc.gov/2020052295
LC ebook record available at https://lccn.loc.gov/2020052296

Contents

Introduction

Welcome to Mathematics and Statistics

*W*elcome to a career in mathematics and/or statistics! If you are interested in a career in this challenging, exciting, rewarding, and versatile field, you've come to the right book! This book is an ideal start for understanding the various careers available to you under the mathematics umbrella. It discusses the paths you should consider following to ensure you have all the training, education, and experience needed to succeed in your future career goals.

You don't have to be Einstein to enjoy a career in mathematics or statistics!
RICHVINTAGE/E+/GETTY IMAGES

Everywhere you look nowadays, you'll hear about the importance of data, the amount of data, uses of big data, and so on. The sheer amount of data that's collected by various devices and analyzed for commercial, medical, or educational uses is astounding. That's good news for people who enjoy working with numbers. Careers in math and stats are growing by leaps and bounds, and they are becoming increasingly interesting and lucrative.

You may be wondering where the line is drawn between mathematicians and statisticians. That line can be blurry, as indicated by the fact that both career paths are covered in this book. However, at their base level, the difference between the two can be described as one between theory and practical applications. While mathematicians are usually concerned with abstract measurement and creating results through functional processing, statisticians prefer a more involved methodology.

Determining the real-world impact of numbers is a core job of a statistician. For a mathematician, whose work is mostly in the realm of the abstract, it's more about representing data in a form that the average nonspecialist can understand.[1]

That said, these professions do blur together often, and many people with degrees in mathematics have long, successful careers as statisticians.

A Career in Mathematics/Statistics

A career in math/stats is almost impossible to describe in just a few sentences, because it can contain such a wide variety of roles, responsibilities, and locations. Here are just a few characteristics of such a career:

- You need to enjoy and excel at mathematics. You should have, or be able to develop, excellent analytical and problem-solving skills.
- You may work with many different kinds of people—people of all ages, experience levels, and roles within the company. You may have to explain concepts and results to people who fear or "hate" math.
- In addition to analytical skills and problem-solving skills, you need good written and oral communication skills. You need to hone your ability

to communicate results and findings to nonstatisticians and people intimidated by math.

- Even though you might be out of college by the time you get your first job, your "education" will never be finished. The world of data and statistics changes often, and professionals in general have to keep educating themselves on the latest technologies throughout their careers.

Interpreting data is only one part of your job—you'll also need to effectively communicate your findings to other employees, clients, and bosses.
ANDREYPOPOV/ISTOCK/GETTY IMAGES

Because math is such a broad career path, there are many different ways to divide it into categories. For simplicity, this book breaks it into five main areas. (Keep in mind that you can ask five different people who do this for a living how to break this career into categories and you'll get five slightly different answers.)

- *Statisticians*: They develop or apply mathematical or statistical theory and methods to collect, organize, interpret, and summarize data. The goal is to provide usable information. They may specialize in fields such as biostatistics or agricultural, business, or economic statistics. We'll discuss several fields in this realm throughout the book.

- *College math professors:* Postsecondary math teachers teach courses pertaining to mathematical concepts, statistics, and actuarial science. Such a position almost always requires a PhD.
- *Actuaries*: They analyze statistical data—such as mortality, accident, sickness, disability, and retirement rates—and create probability tables. The goal is to forecast risk and liability for payment of future benefits. They may also determine insurance rates and calculate cash reserves necessary to pay future benefits.
- *Research analysts:* Operations research analysts create and apply mathematical models to develop and interpret information that helps management with decision-making. Market research analysts research, analyze, interpret, and present data related to markets, operations, economics, customers, and other information related to the field they work in. For example, they may study market conditions to examine potential sales of a product or service.
- *Economists*: They conduct research, prepare reports, or create plans to tackle economic problems related to the production and distribution of goods and services or monetary and fiscal policy. They may collect and process economic data using sampling techniques and methods.[2]

Note that we don't cover careers like accounting, physics, or engineering in this book, since those are typically separate educational paths. They involve a lot of math, but typically require accounting, physics, or engineering degrees.

In addition to the five main job titles described in the book, the sidebar called "A Rose by Any Other Name" lists many, many job titles you might see that are interchangeable with the careers covered in this book.

A ROSE BY ANY OTHER NAME

There are many jobs available to those with mathematics degrees! There are so many that we can't possibly cover them all here. A very similar job can go by many different titles, depending on the industry, the size of the organization, and many other factors. Here's a list of job titles you might see that all tie back to mathematics and statistics.

- Accountant
- Aerospace engineer
- Applications programmer
- Astronomer
- Banking/credit manager
- Biometrician/biostatician
- Commodity trader
- Computer consultant
- Cost estimator/analyst
- Cryptographer
- Data processing manager
- Data scientist
- Estate planner

- External auditor
- Financial auditor
- Financial consultant
- Financial planner
- Investment analyst
- Investment banker
- Market researcher
- Mechanical engineer
- Numerical analyst
- Physicist
- Rate analyst
- Software engineer

So, what are jobs in these areas like? Are jobs in one category only, or is there some overlap? What education, skills, and certifications do you need to succeed in these fields? What are the salary and job outlooks for each category? And what are the pros and cons of each type of math/stats job? This book answers these questions, and many more, in the following chapters.

The Market Today

The mathematics/statistics markets in the United States is in excellent shape, and it will probably remain one of the most stable, productive forces in the US job market for years to come. Between now and 2029, the US Bureau of Labor

Statistics expects the mathematics/statistics job market to grow 33 percent, which is much greater growth than average.[3] In addition, the median salary is also over twice as high as the average income for all jobs.[4]

The "Occupational Outlook Handbook" on the Bureau of Labor Statistics website (www.bls.gov/ooh) has current US information about this profession. Check out www.bls.gov/ooh/math/mathematicians-and-statisticians.htm for more information about the state of this profession in the United States. We will discuss this in further detail in chapter 1.

What Does This Book Cover?

This book takes you through the steps to see if a career in math/stats might be right for you. It also gives you practical advice on how to pursue an education that will set you up to be a successful candidate for the type of job you might want.

- Chapter 1 describes the many specific paths that a mathematics career can take. This chapter gives you an idea of the many different types of career options that exist.
- Chapter 2 describes the education requirements that you should know as you think about entering the mathematics/statistics field. It talks about steps that you can take as early as high school to prepare yourself, and it also describes the things you can do outside of class to help yourself be ready for a mathematics education.
- Chapter 3 looks at educational options that will lead you to a job in math/stats. It discusses academic requirements, costs, and financial aid options that will help you understand your economic options.
- Chapter 4 helps you build the tools that will help you prepare for interviewing for jobs and internships. It also helps with cover letters, explains how to dress for meetings, and helps you understand what employers expect out of people looking for jobs.

Throughout each of the chapters, you'll read interviews with real people, at various stages of their careers, who chose math or stats as a career path. They offer advice, encouragement, and ways to determine if this is something that might be right for you.

"I don't think you can go wrong [majoring in math or stats] if you generally enjoy math. There are a lot of great jobs out there for someone with a math/stats degree. Don't worry about what you will do—there will be great opportunities."—Thomas Allenburg, statistician

Where Do You Start?

Take a breath and jump right into the next chapter. Chapter 1, "Why Choose a Career in Mathematics/Statistics?" will answer lots of questions you might already have, including questions about job availability, salary, and whether your personality is built for a career in math. If you already know that this is the career path you want, it's still a good idea to read the chapter, because it offers insight into specific pros and cons of this field that you might not have considered.

Even if you're not sure about math or stats, keep reading, because the next chapter is going to give you some really good information about the industry. It will break down the many different types of careers within mathematics and will be helpful in determining which area you might find most interesting.

Your future awaits!
TORTOON/ISTOCK/GETTY IMAGES

Why Choose a Career in Mathematics/Statistics?

*I*n the introduction, you learned that mathematics/statistics are growing fields and are expected to be strong career paths for a long time. At the same time, you should understand that these are very competitive industries and that to succeed in them, you'll need to keep learning throughout your career.

This book is not designed to convince you that you should pursue a career in math or stats. Instead, its goal is to thoroughly describe various careers within their realm to help you decide whether they are something you'd like to explore.

The good news is that professionals with mathematics and statistics degrees are hot commodities. Companies are struggling to fill the slots with qualified workers. This means that they're in great demand. You'll learn more about the demand in the field later in this chapter.

This chapter discusses five key fields that were presented in the Introduction. It covers the basic skills and tasks in each. After reading this chapter, you will have a good understanding of five different types of jobs, and you can start to determine if one of them is a good fit for you. Let's get started!

What Do Mathematics Professionals Do?

If you have ever wondered what people actually do with a math degree, you should know that the possibilities are almost endless. People who study mathematics become economists, accountants, statisticians, research analysts, financial planners, math teachers and professors, commodity traders, or computer consultants. They can pursue any number of other careers that require analytical thinking and a mathematical mind.

Mathematicians increasingly find themselves in careers that specialize in, or are complemented by, computer science and big data. They work for large companies, universities, governments, in health and medicine, in government, and in physical and environmental sciences. They may create and maintain software programs that determine trends, track user entries and actions, and predict habits and preferences. If an organization has numbers or data to be mined, used, or manipulated, you can rest assured there are math majors working there. If you still aren't convinced, check out the sidebar in the introduction entitled "A Rose by Any Other Name," which lists some of the many, many careers available to math and statistics majors.

If you enjoy working with numbers, your career opportunities are nearly limitless.
RIDOFRANZ/ISTOCK/GETTY IMAGES

The following is just a sample of the kinds of tasks that math majors in all different careers do:

- Statisticians collect, organize, interpret, and summarize data. They take mountains of data and turn it into usable information.
- Math professors conduct math-related research, such as developing new mathematics to solve unanswered questions, using existing mathematics

to show real-world phenomena, and applying mathematical techniques to assist in solving problems.

- Financial planners help their clients meet their long-term financial goals. They consult with clients to analyze their goals, determine their risk tolerance, and identify good investments for them.
- Accountants prepare and analyze their client's financial records. They manage the financial data, create financial statements, and ensure regulatory compliance with the client's accounting practices.
- Software engineers use their knowledge of engineering and mathematical principles and programming languages to build software products and run network control systems.

This is just an arbitrary sampling of the different kinds of careers and tasks you can have as a mathematics/statistics major. The point is to show you how broad and varied this field is.

The use of math has become so integrated into our lives that it's hard to count how many ways it affects us. That's one of the reasons that the industry offers so many different opportunities and different types of jobs. If you enjoy math, love to know how things work, are detail-oriented by nature, and like a fast-paced environment, a career in math/statistics might be good for you. On the other hand, you may work long hours, and you might need to be on call overnight or during the weekend. There can be a lot of stress, because the success of the company rides on its data. So consider these facets while you learn more.

Here are the five main areas first mentioned in the introduction that we will cover in depth in the book:

- Statisticians (which includes biostatisticians, econometricians, statistical physicists, and actuaries)
- College math professors
- Actuaries
- Research analysts
- Economists

Let's look at each of these in more detail now.

STATISTICIANS

Statisticians use statistical theory and methods to collect, organize, interpret, and summarize data. The goal is to provide usable information and make sense of that information. They may specialize in fields such as biostatistics or agricultural, business, or economic statistics. They find lucrative roles in areas such as business, health and medicine, government, physical sciences, and environmental sciences.

Statisticians often are separated by whether they work with theoretical or applied statistics. Theoretical statisticians may study the theory of inference or sampling, for example. They essentially prove that the methods used by applied statistics are good. Applied statisticians focus on collecting data properly, making sense of it, quantifying error in data measurement, and building models to predict future trends.[1]

Regardless of where a statistician works, their daily tasks are likely to include the following:

- Collecting, analyzing, and interpreting data
- Identifying trends and relationships in data
- Designing processes for data collection
- Communicating findings to stakeholders
- Advocating for certain organizational and business strategies
- Assisting in decision making based on their findings[2]

Skills you need to succeed as a statistician include a sharp eye for detecting patterns and anomalies in data, comfort using computer systems, algorithms, and other technologies, and strong (written and verbal) communication skills so you can effectively communicate your findings to others, many of whom may not have a technical background.

Note: Truly effective statisticians must be able to think critically about the data that they are analyzing through the lens of key stakeholders and executives. Learning to think like a leader can help statisticians identify trends and data points that can make a big difference in their organizations.[3]

HELENA HOEN: BIOSTATISTICIAN

Helena Hoen holds a BS and MS in statistics from Virginia Polytechnic Institute and State University (commonly known as Virginia Tech). She has been a biostatistician for twenty-five years, mostly working with medical schools at several universities. She has also worked in industry—in pharmaceuticals, small biotech, and one contract research organization—and has taught statistics and mathematics to undergraduates at a local college.

Helena Hoen
COURTESY OF HELENA HOEN.

Can you explain how you became interested in statistics as a career path?

I was taking a course in stats as an undergraduate for a teaching degree. Originally, I thought I'd be a math teacher. I found that I loved medical research as a way to apply math. I looked at the *Occupational Outlook Handbook* at the school library and learned more about statistics as a career path. I then changed my major to statistics and took five years to get my undergraduate degree.

Upon receiving my undergraduate degree, I pursued some employment positions. What I found was that, for a bachelor's degree, the salary barely covered the cost of living. Also, what you could do with a bachelor's degree wasn't as compelling or challenging. I determined that I needed at least a master's to get a good job in biostatistics. I think that is still the case in biostatistics today. So, I then went back to Virginia Tech as a master's student.

What's a "typical" day in your job?

I'll describe a typical day working for medical schools, as that has been my longest and most fulfilling career path. Once monthly, we had a department meeting as well as study meetings on an as-needed basis. At these meetings, we would discuss where the study was, where the data collection was, and so on. There are also meetings about statistics only—that would be with me and the investigators. An investigator is the person doing the study, such as a researcher, doctor, graduate student, or epidemiologist, for example.

You may be brought into a study at different stages. The initial work on a project includes grant review and study plan review. You can contribute to the statistical part of that process and about the appropriate data collection process. You may help determine the research questions, as well as determine and implement the methods used.

If data has already been collected, you are sent a dataset and you then play detective. You're looking at the data to clarify it, which includes reviewing the background info (grant and study proposal). The initial stages of analysis include data cleaning, detective work, investigating unusual observations (are they real or mistakes?), exploring the data for structure, and so on.

Then you do the analysis itself. You work with data, properly analyze it, and look for patterns and determine what it's telling you. You write up the data results and methods and share them with the investigators.

The final product is usually an abstract (which have annual deadlines), manuscript (which you review), a published paper (you add review peer review comments that are to do with the statistics), or a presentation. The investigators typically create these, but they use your findings and analysis in those reports.

The hours can be long, because you have to meet strict deadlines, no matter how complex a study or the data ends up being. I often ate lunch at my desk while working.

Can you give examples of the kind of data that biostatisticians deal with?

Applications of biostatistics include data related to diabetes, heart disease, epilepsy in children, pediatric cardiology, heart transplants, orthopedics, etc. You may be looking at different treatments and machines and determining if there is a difference in outcomes. How do you get best outcomes based on treatment protocols? For diabetes, maybe you get three-month HBA1C (blood sugar levels) and fasting glucose levels. You are often comparing different pills, methods, treatments, and so on, and looking at behavioral and physiological outcomes. Sometimes you're even looking at the instruments, such as which heart-monitoring device works better with infants at home. With cancer, you may be studying survival analysis and survival time on each drug, the amount of tumors found, and so on. You are often making some kind of comparison in the research—whether it's between two treatment protocols, methods, drugs, machines, and so on.

How has the job changed in the last twenty years?

In medical schools at least, it's changed a lot with respect to funding. When I started, the NIH (National Institutes of Health) funded a lot more of our research. Over time, those budgets have been sliced and diced. Researchers look toward private industry for funding, which changes the things you have to research for. Profit more often determines what you can research now. Of course, research has always been determined by how many people are affected and how it affects the overall economics involved. But it's certainly worse now.

I think it's an overall negative trend to depend so strongly on industry funding, because the goals can't always be for profit. That's not putting people's well-being as the top priority, which is where it should be, in my opinion.

What's the best part of being in this field?

I like collaborating with investigators, learning about their research questions, and figuring out how to answer their questions using statistics. There are a variety of applications involved, too, which is nice. Programming is a fun part of it as well, and you have to determine how to get it to work and how you can keep using it. You are always learning and growing, which I love.

I also enjoy the network of fellow biostatisticians that you get to know—it's a small enough field that you get to know each other. I like that networking part. I also like that I am contributing to medical science.

What's the most challenging part of this field?

There is a puzzle to figure out, so you have to be comfortable not knowing the answers and having to figure them out. What does the investigator want to learn from their data? They don't always know the questions that they have—they don't always know that. You also need to tell them sometimes that their data wasn't strong enough to answer their question, or that the answer isn't what they want to hear. You have to break it to them kindly.

What kinds of challenges does the field impress upon the people who work in it?

You sometimes are dealing with other people's math anxiety. They might get defensive or don't understand that it takes time to look at data. You have to explain your field and job to people quite often. It's more complex than people realize. It's not formulaic, and many people think it is. Potential biases can affect data, and so on.

Do you think the current education adequately prepares students to enter the field?

Yes, although, if I had known that there was a biostatistics degree at the time, I would have been better prepared. But I did learn the methodology on my own, as I needed to.

To get a good in-depth feel for statistical analysis, you really need a master's degree. You don't have time to get into it very deep with a bachelor's degree—you are getting background info at that point. When I interviewed with a bachelor's, I didn't feel prepared to do analyses. It's too big an area. You might end up doing a lot of the tedious, detailed work.

As a master's holder, you have many different bosses. You have lots of responsibility but not always the authority that you would like.

Where do you see the field going in the future?

There is increasingly more and more data, so it will continue to be a strong job market. It's not going away! Especially in the medical profession with the regulatory requirements, they need people who specialize in the data to do stats.

What traits or skills make for a good statistician?

You have to be detail oriented, for sure. You should have a strong interest in the area of application and have some background knowledge in the area in which you work, such as biology, etc. You have to be flexible, okay with working on multiple projects at a time, have strong communications skills and always strive to be clear, and be a good listener so you know what questions to ask. Be curious!

What advice do you have for young people considering this career?

Does it appeal to you? Give a lot of thought as to whether these challenges sound interesting. Can you be comfortable finding answers; are you okay with pursuing a master's or PhD? Can you secure your own funding? Consider whether you can deal with stress and long hours. It's rewarding, but also challenging and sometimes stressful.

How can a young person prepare for this career while in high school?

Try to shadow if you can, although I don't know if that's possible. Talk to other people who have the job and ask questions. Make sure you enjoy math and take a stats class in high school if you can. Think about the application of statistics, too—take classes in that, such as business, marketing, finance, biology, medicine, psychology, etc.

Any closing comments?

Job security is excellent. The job market is strong. It's better if you're willing to move where the job is. When you go on job interviews, ask questions about the work environment. Are they going to value what you do and your contributions? Will you be supported when you ask questions? Those things will affect your job satisfaction.

COLLEGE MATH PROFESSORS

To be a college-level (postsecondary level) teacher in any discipline, you'll need a PhD in that field. To teach at the elementary or secondary school level (such as high school), teachers typically need a master's degree. This book doesn't cover teaching at the primary and secondary levels (grades 1–12, essentially) because those important jobs have much more in common with teaching in general than with other math careers. If you're interested in teaching at those levels, please check out *Educational Professionals: A Practical Career Guide,* another book in this same series, which discusses the ins and outs of teaching and even includes an interview with an inspirational middle school math teacher.

Unlike with high school teachers, teaching classes is not the primary job of a professor. Professors have many professional responsibilities in addition to teaching. In many university mathematics departments, the responsibilities of a typical tenured or tenure-track faculty member are usually allocated as 40 percent research, 40 percent teaching, and 20 percent service.[4] In addition, the teaching responsibilities include many more activities than just teaching classes.

Professors teach classes at the undergraduate and graduate level. The typical math professor will teach between one and three classes each semester. They also often supervise undergraduate research projects and help advise students who are working on their doctorate degrees, as well as write letters of recommendation for students. All this falls under the umbrella of teaching when you're a university professor.

The service component can include things like serving on committees in the mathematics department or at the university level, writing reviews of published mathematics papers or books, serving as an editor of a mathematics journal, or organizing research conferences.

Some of the tasks math professors might be responsible for under the research umbrella include the following:[5]

- Doing mathematics research, of course. Many people erroneously think that all mathematics is currently known. In fact, there is more mathematics research being done now than at any time in history.[6] Math professors do a variety of things in their research, such as develop new mathematics to solve unanswered questions, use existing mathematics to model real-world phenomena, and apply mathematical techniques to address problems in the physical sciences, medicine, engineering, data analysis, or other fields.

- Writing research results in papers and submitting these papers for publication.
- Writing textbooks that can be used by other researchers or in graduate courses.
- Submitting grant applications to support their research, and administering grants (working with budgets and submitting reports) that have been awarded.
- Traveling to conferences or to other universities to give talks, share research results, and stay current with what is going on in their area of study.
- Supervising a research project or group that contains several postdocs and students.[7]

According to salary.com, math professors make anywhere from $58,000 to $158,000 annually in the United States. The median salary is $102,000.[8]

ACTUARIES

Actuaries use math and statistics to estimate the financial impact of uncertainty and help clients minimize risk. For example, they might help an insurance company determine the risk of providing life insurance to a person of a certain age and gender based on data and demographic information. Of course, an actuary's work varies, depending on the different projects they own and the type of insurance they specialize in.

Most actuaries work for insurance companies, full-time in an office setting. They often work on teams that include professionals in other fields, such as accounting, underwriting, and finance. Actuaries in the insurance industry typically specialize in a specific field of insurance, such as health insurance, life insurance, or property and casualty insurance, for example.

Here are some common tasks that actuaries do:

- Collect data for analysis
- Estimate the likelihood and possible economic cost of an event such as death, sickness, an accident, or a natural disaster

- Design, test, and manage insurance policies, investments, pension plans, and other business strategies to minimize risk and maximize profitability
- Create charts, tables, and reports that explain calculations and proposals
- Explain their findings and proposals to company executives, government officials, shareholders, and clients[9]

Actuarial work is done largely with computers. Actuaries use database software to compile data. They use advanced statistics and modeling software to forecast the probability of an event occurring, the potential costs of the event if it does occur, and whether the insurance company has enough money to pay future claims, for example. [10]

The median salary of an actuary was over $108,000 in 2019, and the profession has a strong employment outlook and projected job growth.[11]

RESEARCH ANALYSTS

As mentioned in the introduction, there are several different kinds of research analysts, depending primarily on *what* exactly you are analyzing. Operations research analysts create and apply mathematical models to develop and interpret information that helps management with decision making. For example, they study cost effectiveness, labor requirements, product distribution, and other factors involved in day-to-day operations.

Market research analysts research, analyze, interpret, and present data related to markets, operations, economics, customers, and other information related to the field in which they work. For example, they may study market conditions to examine potential sales of a product or service, perhaps to help management determine an acceptable price point for the item.[12]

Economic analysts perform research on the economy for a federal agency or a private company. They use large amounts of economic data to develop economic forecasts and models.[13]

Regardless of the industry they work in, research analysts typically perform these basic tasks:[14]

- Monitor and forecast trends
- Measure the effectiveness of programs and strategies
- Formulate and evaluate methods for collecting data, such as surveys, questionnaires, and opinion polls

- Gather data about consumers, competitors, and conditions
- Analyze data using statistical software
- Convert complex data and findings into understandable tables, graphs, and written reports
- Prepare reports and present results to clients and management[15]

Most analysts have degrees in technical or quantitative fields, such as engineering, computer science, analytics, and mathematics. Regardless of your major, you'll need extensive coursework in mathematics, including statistics, calculus, and linear algebra.

ECONOMISTS

Economists also do research, collect and analyze data, monitor economic trends, and develop forecasts. Their research, however, often focuses on topics such as energy costs, interest rates, inflation, prices of goods and services, rent trends, imports, or employment. A full quarter of those employed as economists in the United States work for the government.[16]

Some economists study how society distributes resources, such as land, labor, raw materials, and machinery, to produce goods and services.[17] Their focus is on evaluating economic issues (such as scarcity) for such resources, goods, and services.

The economist's day-to-day tasks typically involve the following:

- Researching economic issues, such as recession, inflation, scarcity, and environmental issues
- Conducting surveys and collecting data
- Analyzing data using mathematical models, statistical techniques, and software
- Presenting research results in understandable reports, tables, and charts
- Interpreting and forecasting market trends
- Educating businesses, governments, and individuals about economic topics
- Recommending solutions to economic problems
- Writing articles for academic journals and other media[18]

Research analysts prepare reports or create plans to tackle economic or corporate problems.
DEAGREEZ/ISTOCK/GETTY IMAGES

Note that, in the United States, most economists have a master's degree or PhD. However, some entry-level jobs (primarily in the federal government) are available for economists with bachelor's degrees. The median annual wage for economists was $105,020 in 2019.[19]

Educational Requirements

For most jobs in a "general" math/stats field, the ideal candidate will have a bachelor's (four-year) or master's (six-year) degree in mathematics. Bachelor's degrees in mathematics can be a BS (bachelor of science) or a BA (bachelor of arts). A BS in mathematics provides broad knowledge of mathematics topics with depth in certain areas, while a BA in mathematics provides a solid mathematics core within a flexible curriculum.[20]

In addition to straight math degrees, there are also degrees you can think of as being "heavy on math," such as bachelor's or master's in statistics, accounting, engineering, computer science, physics, biology, chemistry, and astronomy.

If you know you are interested in something in this "math family," deciding which degree path to follow should primarily be determined by your interests. These are all desirable, lucrative, in-demand fields, so you can't go wrong. That said, choosing a math degree can provide you with a breadth and depth of learning and theory that you may not get with other degrees.

As to whether you need education beyond the four-year bachelor's degree, well, that's certainly more likely to be the case than in other fields. Depending on where you work or what your career goals are, it might require you to get a graduate or other advanced degree. For example, many practicing biostatisticians explain that it's difficult to succeed in biostatistics without a master's degree, simply because you need a certain depth of knowledge to understand the complexities of that field. And, if you want to work in academia as a professor or researcher, you will be expected to have a PhD. As you read earlier, most economists also have degrees beyond a bachelor's degree. In sum, the answer to this question depends in part on the area of math you're studying and the field in which you want to work.

As with most technical careers, regardless of your initial education level, it will very likely be necessary to continue pursuing additional education throughout your career. Whatever your interest, do your homework and research your best plan of attack, so you don't waste your time (and money!) going down the wrong path. Chapter 3 describes the educational paths to consider in much more detail.

Job Outlook and Compensation

There are a great many opportunities for anyone interested in mathematics/statistics. These professions continue to grow, due to our increasing reliance on more and more data and on computers in general, as well as our increasing connectedness with the larger world and the amount of useful and valuable data that is stored electronically. Computers can collect data and run programs on it, but it's up to the analytical among us to really make sense of the output.

We will continue to need experienced, smart, curious people who want to continue to collect and interpret data. In fact, the need for mathematicians and statisticians is expected to grow up to 33 percent in the United States through 2029.[21] This is over four times the expected growth of the average occupation (7 percent).[22]

These statistics show just how promising this career is now and in the foreseeable future:

- *Education*—Master's degree
- *2019 median pay*—$92,030 (over twice the average income for all jobs)
- *Job outlook 2019—2029:* 33 percent (much faster than average)
- *Work environment*—Work in the federal government and in private science and engineering research companies. They may work on teams with engineers, scientists, and other professionals.[23]

WHAT IS A MEDIAN INCOME?

Throughout this book, you'll see the term "median income" used frequently. What does it mean? Some people believe it's the same thing as "average income," but that's not correct. While the median income and average income might sometimes be similar, they are calculated in different ways.

The true definition of median income is the income at which half of the workers earn more than that income, and the other half of workers earn less. If this is complicated, think of it this way: Suppose there are five specialists in a company, each with varying skills and experience. Here are their salaries:

- $42,500
- $48,250
- $51,600
- $63,120
- $86,325

What is the median income? In this case, the median income is $51,600, because of the five total positions listed, it is in the middle. Two salaries are higher than $51,600, and two are lower.

The "average income" is simply the total of all salaries, divided by the number of total jobs. In this case, the average income is $58,359.

Why does this matter? The median income is a more accurate way to measure the various incomes in a set because it's less likely to be influenced by extremely high or low numbers in the total group of salaries. For example, in our example of five incomes, the highest income ($86,325) is much higher than the other incomes, and therefore it makes the average income ($58,359) higher than most incomes in the group. Therefore, if you base your income expectations on the average, you'll likely be disappointed to eventually learn that many incomes are below it.

But if you look at median income, you'll always know that half the people are above it, and half are below it. That way, depending on your level of experience and training, you'll have a better estimate of where you'll end up on the salary spectrum.

The Pros and Cons of Being in Mathematics

As you've learned in this chapter, this industry is healthy and poised for growth. Its salaries are generally higher than in other fields, and its expected growth is higher than in many other occupations.

The list of pros of being in mathematics/statistics is long, but here are some of the highlights. Consider these benefits as you think about whether it's a good fit for you:

- Good salaries
- Large growth in these industries over the next decade
- Dynamic, rapidly changing environment to keep you interested
- Interesting people with whom to work
- Demand in nearly every type of organization and anywhere you would want to live

- Ability to never stop learning
- Job can be completely remote
- Traveling opportunities are abundant
- Because job cultures vary greatly, you can find one that fits you
- Many different specialties exist in mathematics, which translates to plentiful career and promotion options

Note: According to the National Association of Colleges and Employers annual salary survey, math majors make an average of almost 40 percent more than English, history, sociology, and psychology majors.[24]

Not everything about mathematics is favorable. Like most industries, it has its share of downsides. The following is a list of cons of working in the mathematics/statistics arena:

- Long hours
- Hectic pace
- Increasing competition from other countries
- Constant need to stay current with technologies, theories, and methodologies
- Mentally taxing and challenging
- Lack of diversity within staff

Regarding diversity, members of the industry seem encouraged that the diversity issue is slowly getting better, and that succeeding in mathematics/statistics in general is headed toward more of a merit-focused status. In other words, their hope is that we're headed toward an environment in which earning and keeping a good career is based on how well you perform—as opposed to your ethnicity, gender, age, or some other aspect that has nothing to do with job performance.

THOMAS ALLENBURG: THE BUSINESS OF STATISTICS

Thomas Allenburg
COURTESY OF THOMAS ALLENBURG.

Thomas Allenburg received a bachelor of science degree in mathematics at St. Olaf College with a concentration in statistics. He then received a master's degree in statistics from Virginia Polytechnic Institute and State University (commonly known as Virginia Tech). His first job was working for the University of Minnesota in Biostatistics—he helped with clinical trials for a new AIDS drug. When funding fell through, he moved to a marketing company as a statistician for their catalog and direct mail efforts. He then worked at AT&T, doing targeted database marketing. He also worked for Carlson Marketing Group, the largest loyalty marketing agency in the world at the time. He managed airline frequent flyer programs, Hallmark's Gold Crown program, and other customer loyalty programs. He was there eight years. His current position is with United Healthcare, specifically focusing on the Medicare population. They use data to enroll people into their Medicare plans. He's held that job for seventeen years.

Can you explain how you became interested in statistics as a career path?

I ended up in math in college because it was fairly easy to me. I got some great advice freshman year from an adviser—major in something you enjoy! I was doing poorly in chemistry but loving calculus. So, I was a math major because I enjoyed it. I took a few statistics classes and I liked the practical application of math to solving problems. There were also programs that recruited students to go into statistics (such as graduate programs with assistantships). I decided late to pursue the master's, and it was a practical decision, too, because I got to go to graduate school free.

What's a "typical" day in your job?

At this point in my career, I am not doing stats every day. I have a team of 130 people doing the actual work. At this level, I am in a management role. I meet with our internal customers and make sure we are meeting their needs. I help train and grow our talent, too.

Your standard statistician in marketing attempts to use data to better personalize the communications with members as well as intelligently reach out to perspective members. Day to day, they work closely with internal stakeholders, such as ad marketers planning to send out mailings or emails, to determine who the audience is and what questions we want to answer.

They might then use regression analysis and predictive models to determine who will likely respond to this kind of outreach. They sift through hundreds of attributes to build a statistical model. They also measure effectiveness of the dollars we spend. They get involved setting up experiments to get the best results and measure how different tactics work.

We use our customer database with members and former members as well as licensed data from third parties—census, surveys, public records, etc. We marry that information to known behaviors of people that are our members.

How has the job changed in the last twenty years?

It has changed a lot, because communication is so different now. Digital communication is the main way we communicate with customers. The data is also ever changing.

Also, because the world is becoming more digital, there is so much more data. Big data! We now analyze tens of millions of records instead of thirty, for example. The volume of data is immense and the approach has to be different.

We also need more powerful computing power, so there is a more direct connection to IT than ever before. Having an IT background with statistics is very useful.

What's the best part of being in this field?

I like the ability to measure what I've done. If we develop analytics and use them, we can actually quantify their value. The ability to set up an experiment and prove your worth, so to speak, is really rewarding.

What's the most challenging part of this field?

For someone who goes into stats, you are analytical and concerned about methodology and details. But often you are doing this work on behalf of people who are not oriented that way. So you have to take complexity and translate it into something simple that you can explain to others. How do you boil this complex relationship down to one PowerPoint slide?

Communicating these complex ideas clearly and simplifying them is a challenge. The communications element is as important as the stats itself—writing ability, graphic design skills (compelling visuals), the ability to marry storytelling and visualization. People who can do those well really excel.

Do you think the current education adequately prepares students to enter the field?

From what I have observed, there are now more programs available, like data science majors, that are bringing together statistics and technology—which is good.

The emergence of these new programs is an attempt to meet more modern needs, so that's good. Even in the last five years, there have been changes in this regard.

Where do you see the field going in the future?

Information technology programs might almost be taking over statistics in a way. There are more and more tools and technologies based on statistics, but have a new vernacular driven by IT and the big data phenomenon. I think that will get more and more blurry. I think getting a technology background will become even more important, if not crucial. Anything involving data is growing in importance and it's not going away. It's a very safe career to pursue. Demand will increase.

What traits or skills make for a good statistician?

You must have an aptitude for math, to begin with. With statistics, it's an applied science. You are performing work on behalf of others. There is a consulting element to this job. So you really need people skills, too! You have to understand from others what they really need even if they don't know how to explain it. You have to translate it for them. Listening and understanding are key skills. Also, you have to take something that's complex and explain it in a way that's simple. That's a very great skill to have and it *can* be acquired over time through experience.

What advice do you have for young people considering this career?

I don't think you can go wrong here if you generally enjoy math. There are a lot of great jobs out there for someone with a math/stats degree. Don't worry about what you will do—there will be great opportunities. You used to need a graduate degree in statistics, but that might not be the case anymore, at least in a business setting. In a business direction, there is more being offered at the undergrad level and so much more automation through technology. You can get a pretty good job with a bachelor's, but generally a master's degree is better. The depth of understanding is better. Having an IT background in addition to math or stats is also very helpful.

How can a young person prepare for this career while in high school?

It's always a good idea to network and take advantage of connections. Go talk to people. See what the job is actually like and ask good questions. Talk to people with real-world experience. Also, don't assume that everyone in the field has a similar job. There are lots of different jobs out there—research and medicine, using stats in manufacturing—that are all very different. There are a lot of flavors of jobs and the jobs are very different.

═══════════════

Would I Be a Good Mathematician/Statistician?

This is a tough question to answer, because really the answer can only come from you. But don't despair! There are plenty of resources both online and elsewhere that can help you find the answer. They guide you through the types of questions and considerations that will bring you to your conclusion.

Of course, no job is going to match your personality or fit your every desire, especially when you are just starting out. There are, however, some aspects to a job that may be so unappealing or simply mismatched that you may decide to opt for something else, or equally you may be so drawn to a feature of a job that any downsides are not that important.

Obviously, having an ability and a passion for mathematics and for working with numbers in general is one of the keys to success in this field, but there are

Picking a career you enjoy and can excel at is key to your future happiness.
VASYL DOLMATOV/ISTOCK/GETTY IMAGES

other factors to keep in mind. One way to see if you may be cut out for this career is to ask yourself the following questions:

- *Am I a highly curious and tenacious person who enjoys solving problems?*
  You need a real curiosity for the profession and enjoy learning from your mistakes, as well as be open to learning new things. You have to be willing to work at a problem until you find a solution, and not easily give up. Excellent problem-solving skills are a must.

- *Can I think critically and build complex mental models of the systems I am working with?*
  You need to be able to think analytically. You should have, or be able to develop, excellent analytical and problem-solving skills.

- *Can I communicate complex ideas effectively to others?*
  Communication is a key skill to have in any profession, but particularly here. You need to be able to take complicated and complex findings and trends and explain them to people who may not have the acuity for numbers you have. If you don't like teaching others, this is not for you. This includes both written and oral communication.

- *Am I willing to continue learning at all times and have a passion for numbers and data?*
  If you can continue to learn from others, you can continue to hone your skill set. You also have to be passionate about it. It's more of a lifestyle than just a career.

Note: Although it's one thing to *read* about the pros and cons of a particular career, the best way to really get a feel for what a typical day is like on the job and what the challenges and rewards are is to talk to someone who is working in the profession. You can also learn a lot by reading the interviews with actual mathematicians and statisticians that you find sprinkled throughout this book.

If the answer to any of these questions is an adamant no, you might want to consider a different path. Remember that learning what you *don't* like can be just as important and figuring out what you do like to do.

Summary

Most of this chapter was devoted to describing the different types of mathematics jobs and a little bit about them:

- Statisticians
- College math professors
- Actuaries
- Research analysts
- Economists

The chapter went into detail on each job type, including example jobs within each category, the job outlook, whether demand for that job is expected to grow in the near future, the educational requirements, and the compensation you can expect.

One important point to remember from this chapter is that there are many diverse types of jobs in math, in nearly every type of business imaginable. So if there is any industry in which your opportunities are nearly limitless, mathematics is probably it.

Chapter 2 explores how to build a plan for your future. It discusses everything from educational requirements and certifications to internship opportunities within the industry. You'll learn about finding summer jobs and making the most of volunteer work as well. While mathematics/statistics jobs are numerous, the industry is quite competitive. This chapter will discuss how you can set yourself apart from the crowd.

Forming a Career Plan

Now that you have some idea what careers in mathematics and statistics look like, and maybe you even know which branch of it you are interested in, it's time to formulate a career plan. For you organized folks out there, this can be a helpful and energizing process. If you're not a naturally organized person, or perhaps the idea of looking ahead and building a plan to adulthood scares you, you are not alone. That's what this chapter is for.

After we talk about ways to develop a career plan (there is more than one way to do this!), the chapter dives into the educational requirements. Finally, we will look at how you can gain experience in your community. Yes, experience will look good on your résumé, and in some cases it's even required. But even more important, getting out there and working with in various settings is the best way to determine if mathematics/statistics is really something that you enjoy. When you find a career that you truly enjoy and have a passion for, it will rarely feel like work at all.

If you still aren't sure if this field is right for you, try a self-assessment questionnaire or a career aptitude test. There are many good ones on the web. As an example, the career-resource website monster.com includes its favorite free self-assessment tools at https://www.monster.com/career-advice/article/best -free-career-assessment-tools. The Princeton Review also has a very good aptitude test geared toward high schoolers at www.princetonreview.com/quiz/career-quiz.

Tip: Check out the site https://thisisstatistics.org/quiz/ to take a quiz written by the American Statistical Association called "What Kind of Statistician Could You Be?" You answer five simple questions, and it shows you which area of statistics best matches your interests and personal tastes. Possible results include biostatistician, data journalist, data analyst, data scientist, and more.

This chapter could just as well have been titled "How to Not End Up Miserable at Work." Because really, what all this is about is achieving happiness. After all, unless you're independently wealthy, you're going to have to work. That's just a given. If you work for 8 hours a day, starting at 18 and retiring at 65, you're going to spend around 100,000 hours at work. That's about eleven years. Your life will be much, *much* better if you find a way to spend that time doing something you enjoy, that your personality is suited for, and that your skills help you become good at. Plenty of people don't get to do that, and you can often see it in their faces as you go about your day interacting with other people who are working. In all likelihood, they did not plan their careers very well and just fell into a random series of jobs that were available.

So, your ultimate goal should be to match your personal interests/goals with your preparation plan for college/careers. Practice articulating your plans and goals to others. Once you feel comfortable voicing your career aspirations, that means you have a good grasp of your goals and the plan to reach them.

What Are *You* Like?

Every good career plan begins with you. A good place to start is by thinking about your own qualities. What are you like? Where do you feel comfortable and where do you feel uncomfortable? Ask yourself the questions in the box called "All About You" and then think about how your answers match up with mathematics.

ALL ABOUT YOU

Personality Traits

- Are you introverted or extroverted?
- How do you react to stress? Do you stay calm when others panic?
- Do you prefer people or technology and machinery?
- Are you more creative or more analytical?
- Are you better at making things or explaining things?
- Are you organized or creative, or a little of both (or neither)?

- How much money do you want to make—just enough or all of it?
- What does the word "success" mean to you?

Interests

- Are you interested in how things work?
- Are you interested in solving problems?
- Are you interested in helping people?
- Are you interested in moving up a clear career ladder?
- Or would you like to move around from one kind of job to another?

Likes and Dislikes

- Do you like to figure things out or to know ahead of time exactly what's coming up?
- Do you like working on your own or as part of a team?
- Do you like talking to people or do you prefer minimal interaction?
- Do you like to figure out problems and solve them?
- Can you take direction from a boss or teacher, or do you want to decide for yourself how to do things?
- Do you like things to be the same or to change a lot?

Strengths and Challenges

- What is something you accomplished that you're proud of?
- Are you naturally good at school or do you have to work harder at some subjects?
- Are you physically strong and active, or not so much?
- Are you flexible and able to adapt to changes and new situations?
- Are you better at math or better at English?
- Are you better at computers or doing things with your hands?
- What is your best trait (in your opinion)?
- What is your worst trait (in your opinion)?

Remember, this list is for only for you. You're not trying to impress anybody or tell anyone what you think they want to hear. You're just talking to you. Be as honest as you can—tell yourself the truth, not what you think someone else would want the answer to be. Once you have a good list about your own interests, strengths, challenges, likes and dislikes, you'll be in a better position to know what kind of career you want.

ABOUT THE JOB

- What kind of work will you be doing?
- What kind of environment will you be working in?
- Will you have regular nine-to-five hours, or will you be working evenings, weekends, and overtime?
- What kind of community would you be living in: city, suburb, or small town?
- Will you be able to live where you want to? Or will you need to go where the job is?
- Will you work directly with customers or clients?
- What will your coworkers be like?
- How much education will you need?
- Do you need certifications?
- Is there room for advancement?
- What does the job pay?
- What kind of benefits will the job provide (if any)?
- Is there room to change jobs and try different things?

Planning the Plan

In this chapter, you are on a fact-finding mission of sorts. A career fact-finding plan, no matter what the field, should include these main steps:

- Take some time to consider and jot down your interests and personality traits, with the previous sections' help.
- Find out as much as you can about the day-to-day of mathematicians and statisticians at all levels. In what kinds of environments do they

work? Who will you work with? How demanding is the job? What are the challenges? Chapter 1 of this book is designed to help you in this regard.

- Find out about educational requirements and schooling expectations. Will you be able to meet any rigorous requirements?
- Seek out opportunities to volunteer or shadow others doing the job. Use your critical thinking skills to ask questions and consider whether this is the right environment for you. This chapter also discusses ways to find job-shadowing opportunities and other job-related experiences.
- Look into student aid, grants, scholarships, and other ways you can get help to pay for schooling. It's not just about student aid and scholarships, either. Some larger organizations will pay employees to go back to school to get further degrees.
- Build a timetable for taking required exams such as the SAT and ACT, applying to schools, visiting schools, and making your decision. You should write down all important deadlines and have them at the ready when you need them.
- Continue to look for employment that matters during your college years—internships and work experiences that help you build hands-on experience and knowledge about your actual career.
- Find a mentor who is currently working in your field of interest. This person can be a great source of information, education, and connections. Don't expect a job (at least not at first); just build a relationship with someone who wants to pass along his or her wisdom and experience. Coffee meetings or even emails are a great way to start.

The whole point of career planning is not to overwhelm you with a seemingly huge endeavor; it's to maximize happiness. Your ultimate goal should be to match your personal interests/goals/abilities with your preparation plan for college/careers. Practice articulating your plans and goals to others. Once you feel comfortable doing this, that means you have a good grasp of your goals and the plan to reach them.

A mentor can help you in many ways.
FILADENDRON/E+/GETTY IMAGES

YOUR PASSIONS, ABILITIES, AND INTERESTS: IN JOB FORM!

Think about how you've done at school and how things have worked out at any temporary or part-time jobs you've had so far. What are you really good at, in your opinion? And what have other people told you you're good at? What are you not very good at right now, but you would like to become better at? What are you not very good at, and you're okay with not getting better at?

Now forget about work for a minute. In fact, forget about needing to ever have a job again. You won the lottery—congratulations. Now answer these questions: What are your favorite three ways of spending your time? For each one of those things, can you describe why you think you in particular are attracted to it? If you could get up tomorrow and do anything you wanted all day long, what would it be? These questions can be fun, but can also lead you to your true passions. The next step is to find the job that sparks your passions.

WHERE TO GO FOR HELP

If you're aren't sure where to start, your local library, school library, and guidance counselor office are great places to begin.

VISIT THE GUIDANCE COUNSELOR OFFICE

Each school and each state handles things a little differently, but a high school guidance office will usually have several resources for you, including help for applying to college. Some of the resources you might find in your high school guidance office include the following:

- Seniors handbook
- Higher education handbook
- College visit forms
- Student brag sheet/résumé forms
- Useful links for college planning and searches
- Useful links for scholarships/financial resources
- NCAA hints for sports scholarships
- SAT and ACT information
- Common App tips and application
- Essay writing tips

Your guidance office can also help you take interest and aptitude tests, so you can narrow down your interests or discover new ideas for you've never thought of. They can help you develop a résumé and a career portfolio to show what you've done and what you're capable of. Your guidance counselor can work with you individually; they also put on school-wide or grade-wide workshops, classes, focus groups, or presentations about job skills and personal development.

Make an appointment with a counselor or email them and ask about taking career interest questionnaires. With a little prodding, you'll be directed to lots of good information online and elsewhere.

DO THE RESEARCH YOURSELF

Of course, a well-stocked guidance office or school library/media center will have books like this one for you to explore! You can also start your research with these four sites:

- The Bureau of Labor Statistics' Career Outlook site at http://www.bls .gov/careeroutlook/home.htm. The United States Department of Labor's Bureau of Labor Statistics site doesn't just track job statistics, as you learned in chapter 1. There is an entire portion of this site dedicated to young adults looking to uncover their interests and match those interests with jobs currently in the market. There is a section called "Career Planning for High Schoolers" that you should check out. Information is updated based on career trends and jobs in demand, so you'll get practical information as well.
- The Mapping Your Future site at http://www.mappingyourfuture.org helps you determine a career path and then helps you map out a plan to reach those goals. It includes tips on preparing for college, paying for college, job hunting, résumé writing, and more.
- The Education Planner site at http://www.educationplanner.org has separate sections for students, parents, and counselors. It breaks down the task of planning your career goals into simple, easy-to-understand steps. You can find personality assessments, get tips for preparing for school, learn from some Q&As from counselors, download and use a planner worksheet, read about how to finance your education, and more.
- TeenLife at http://www.teenlife.com calls itself "the leading source for college preparation" and it includes lots of information about summer programs, gap year programs, community service, and more. They believe that spending time out "in the world" outside of the classroom can help students do better in school, find a better fit in terms of career, and even interview better with colleges. This site contains lots of links to volunteer and summer programs.

Use these sites as jumping-off points, but don't be afraid to reach out to a real person, such as a guidance counselor or your favorite teacher, if you're feeling overwhelmed.

TALK TO PROFESSIONALS IN THE FIELD

After you've done some research on your own, you'll already have an idea of which field appeals to you most. But what is it like to really do that job?

One of the best ways to learn what a job is like is to talk to someone who does it. Start with your own city or town. Mathematicians and statisticians are found in every business, university, and governmental body where you live. Ask people you know for introductions to people they know. Or just look them up online and contact them yourself. Even if those people are farther away, there are ways to see these careers through their eyes. Consider these avenues to connect with professionals in the field:

- *Informational interviews*—These can be in person, on the phone, or online via Skype, Zoom, or a similar program. Ask to speak to the person for twenty or thirty minutes. It's important to respect that they are likely to be very busy, and it may be difficult for them to spare you even that much time. Ask them open-ended questions about the job itself, how they chose it, what they like and don't like. Be sure to ask the two most important questions at the end:
  - What other advice would you give me?
  - Who else should I talk to?
- *Job shadowing*—This is an opportunity to spend a day with a professional in order to learn about a career and observe daily work activities. This kind of program is usually organized by your high school guidance office or sometimes through a community program like Junior Achievement.
- *Summer internship programs*—These opportunities can provide a high school student with valuable professional development, mentoring, and job shadowing alongside hands-on work. Check out the further resources section in this book for more information about internships for high school students interested in mathematics and statistics.

SEAN FAHEY: THE MATHEMATICS OF VOTING

Sean Fahey
COURTESY OF SEAN FAHEY.

Sean Fahey received a bachelor of science in mathematics from Wabash College, with a minor in physics, and a master of business administration (MBA) at Indiana University. He worked for over thirteen years in state government for the state of Indiana in a variety of capacities, ranging from an entry-level accountant to an appointment by the governor to run an agency dealing with technology in government. He then entered the private consulting space and currently works for an IT service provider called Quest as a service delivery manager. He manages accounts for several secretaries of state, primarily in the election space—focused on voter registrations. His primary accounts are Indiana, New Hampshire, and Vermont, but he runs the election operations center that spans eleven different accounts.

Can you explain how you became interested in mathematics as a career path?

Math always came easy to me. I was lucky to attend an elementary school where you could work at your own pace. I would work through all the books very quickly. My brain was just wired that way. I enjoyed it, too. I took accelerated classes in high school and in college. Honestly, I didn't give much forethought into how I would apply it to an actual job or career.

I had an experience early on that sent me on a path of science and math. I wrote a composition and the teacher failed me because she said it was "too good" and I must have plagiarized it. That was really upsetting to me. I realized then that a teacher couldn't question numbers—facts are facts. No one could accuse me of not being good at math when I did well in it. I liked the certainty of it. That really did influence what I wanted to do.

What's a "typical" day in your job?

My job is all about problem solving. Sometimes I don't know what the problem is until that day. I hear from a client or from someone on the team about a problem, and my job is to point them in the right direction or help them solve the problem. It involves organizing different teams and keeping track of deadlines and target dates.

For example, absentee voting was a big deal during the COVID-19 crisis. There is typically a list of prescribed reasons you can vote absentee, and different states have different requirements and procedures for allowing absentee voting. In the 2020 primary in Indiana, however, anyone could vote absentee. You didn't need a specific reason. So, we had to create an online form for voters that would allow the election division to verify voter eligibility and then send the ballot to the proper place—we went from an idea, to development, to testing, to release in about three weeks! You could request a ballot online and get it sent to you electronically in a few hours. That was a first.

We are always looking at how to make the technology easier for the voter and for the system (the election division) to use properly. A different state sent out ballots to every voter and we needed to record those that were sent out. We had to write a script to consume that data so voters could see the information on their public portal. It's about logically breaking down a challenge and figuring out how to achieve an outcome.

How has your job changed in the last fifteen years?

Technology has been the biggest change. People can work anywhere, anytime now. You are on call 24/7 because everyone has a cell phone. There are no "typical" office hours. The way that people work together has expanded geographically. You can work with people all over the place—in fact, my team is spread out all over the country. Also, there is a certain expectation that people have technical acumen now.

What's the best part of your job?

I have a direct impact on voters, which I really like. The same was true when I worked in state government, because what we were doing had a positive impact on people's lives. I get a lot of enjoyment out of that aspect of it.

What's the most challenging part of your job?

There are a lot of stakeholders—clients and company both. You have multiple "bosses" and they all might have different agendas, outcomes, and time lines. They might pull you in different directions, which can be challenging.

What's been the most surprising part of your career?

The diversity of the jobs I've held has surprised me. I have been able to do a lot of different things for different departments and industries. I have worked in transportation, for the department of natural resources, in IT, in economic development, and with state election officials. I have always enjoyed being exposed to something that

I didn't know about before. I love the learning all these different aspects and I also had a skill set that they didn't have. Both sides benefited.

Do you think the current education adequately prepares students to enter mathematics?

No, because people put too much emphasis on what happens in the classroom only. Kids are shaped as much by their environment—friends, family, and other influences. I am a strong believer in liberal arts, because it creates a more well-rounded person. If you are put in a track and asked to memorize facts, you are missing the real benefit of education. Regurgitating facts isn't a great education. Simple rote memorization doesn't benefit students and help them function well in the world. Instead, we should be teaching kids to come up with new ideas or change ideas in school. I think that's where liberal arts succeeds better than some other fields.

Going to college doesn't mean you will definitely be a benefit to society. Also, college isn't right for everyone—technical educations and careers are good, too.

What can you do with a math degree? It took me a while to connect math to the job market. What I learned was that studying math helps you to think logically, regardless of what you are doing. You approach the world in this structured way— organized and fact-based. A math degree helps you approach challenges and issues in life in a structured way that helps you solve them.

Where do you see the mathematics field going in the future?

To a certain extent, math is math. I have been reading about theoretical mathematics and physics—which is where the field is evolving. It's interesting to read about where math and science are going, when it seems in some ways very solid and unchanging. It's a known quantity. The career choices and options continue to rise—the economy is looking for problem-solvers who can apply logic to a problem or issue.

What traits or skills make for a good mathematician?

You need good decision-making skills even when you don't have all the information that would be perfect for making that decision. You need a logical and trained mind to make good decisions with imperfect information. You can make better decisions and make them more quickly.

You need to be able to communicate and work well with a team. Verbal and written communication skills are important. Having said that, there are people who are off the charts in math abilities yet who have challenges communicating well with others. Social interaction can be a challenge, but you can work on it and get better.

What advice do you have for young people considering this career?

You will always use it! I actually do use math every day. I use the theories behind math daily. In every problem you approach, you will find application in any career path. It will also set you apart from others. The general logical approach to problem solving is invaluable.

How can a young person prepare for this career while in high school?

Find things that you like to do, regardless of its relationship to math. Having a foundation in mathematics will make you better at whatever you want to do. Get exposure to different careers. If you are interested in the topics, that goes a long way. The application of math should interest you as well.

Any closing comments?

Another great thing about math is that it helps me communicate with others with different skill sets. I can communicate with accountants, for example, because of my math background. I can intelligently discuss code issues with database administrators. No, I can't write code, but I can follow the logic and I understand what the rules well enough to help find the outcome we all want. Approaching things from a math viewpoint can make things more efficient. You can go in and communicate with all kinds of people who have only studied that single discipline. You can look at it from a different angle or approach and do it more efficiently.

Making High School Count

Regardless of the career you choose, there are some basic yet important things you can do while in high school to position yourself in the most advantageous way. Remember—it's not just about having the best application; it's also about figuring out which areas of mathematics or statistics you actually would enjoy doing and which ones don't suit you. Consider these steps toward becoming a well-rounded and marketable person during your high school years:

- Volunteer at your high school or local library's help desk.
- Sign up to be a math tutor at your school or local library.
- Take as many math, programming, and computer classes as possible during your high school career.

- Take speech, communication, debate, and English classes, in order to hone your written and oral communication skills. You'll need them to speak with everyone from coworkers to clients and bosses.
- Use the summers to get as much experience working with numbers as you can. Be comfortable using all kinds of computer software.
- Learn first aid and CPR. You'll need these important skills regardless of your profession.
- Volunteer in as many settings as you can.

CLASSES TO TAKE IN HIGH SCHOOL

High school is a good time to take as many electives and special-interest classes as you can, because doing so will give you a feeling for what you like and don't like, and it will give you experience that you can use as a stepping-stone to find internships and other positions. If your high school is on the small side, you might not have access to all the options listed here, but take what you can. It will build your portfolio and help you discover where your passions lie within mathematics.

- Math of all types, including algebra, geometry, trigonometry, and calculus
- Basic word processing
- Statistics
- Computer science
- Computer programming
- Media technology
- Speech and/or debate

Taking many classes offered by the mathematics department will also give you the opportunity to get to know the instructors who teach those classes. These are people who have likely worked, or currently work, in the fields they teach, which means they have connections and can teach you about the field outside the classroom, as well. Note that many colleges look for comments or recommendations from teachers when considering an application. Building good relationships with your teachers can be a great way to improve your chances of positive recommendations.

Educational Requirements

A mathematics or statistics bachelor's degree can be great for many reasons, and can lead to very successful and lucrative careers. However, this career path will most likely require you to get a graduate or some other advanced degree, if not immediately, then soon after you begin your career.

Most people in mathematics-related fields have advanced degrees, such as master's and PhDs in engineering, business, finance, education, computer science, statistics, economics, and so on. The complexity and level of knowledge required to be a successful statistician, analyst, economist, actuary, and so on require a fuller and more robust educational background. Practically speaking, having a master's degree will most likely place you into a better entry-level position, which will likely include a higher starting salary.

These rigorous educational expectations are not meant to discourage you, however. STEM majors in general, and math majors specifically, are some of the most highly recommended majors for new college students, as those fields are growing and expanding every day.

If you decide to major in mathematics, you should also plan on taking electives and survey classes that provide job-specific skills that can be applied to graduate school or to a specific career, such as accounting, engineering, finance, and various statistics classes. In other words, take time during your undergraduate experience to hone your specific interests in math and focus on taking classes that apply mathematics to that area specifically.

Even though part of your education should be specific to your career path and should involve knowledge of your specific area of interest, such as statistics, for example, having a mathematics degree alone is highly desirable. It shows employers that you have analytical proficiency, knowledge of math theory and practical applications, and problem-solving skills that are highly valued by public and private companies in every industry, including finance, computer and data science, and biotechnology.[1] In short, having a mathematics degree makes you highly sought after.

Be sure to check out chapter 3, which covers the search for the right higher-ed education in more detail.

Keeping your knowledge and education up to date is always important.
ISTOCK/GETTY IMAGES

"Programming skills are important, and you need a good math background of course. The most important thing that people don't really think of as they go through school are communications skills. You have to talk to researchers and find out what they really want. You need to help them be clear about what they really want from a study. That is part of our role, to educate them about what can be done with their data. Communication skills are undervalued but really important in this job." —George Eckert, statistician

Large or Small Company?

What kind of company do you want to work for? And how do you decide? There are opportunities for math/stats professionals at every scale.

Large companies and small companies have both similarities and differences. Whether those qualities are pros or cons depends on you and what you want out of your work experience. Let's compare a few differences.

LARGE COMPANIES

Large companies have the following pros and cons:

- *Structure*—Larger companies tend to have more organization in their organization. There's probably a clear hierarchical structure as well as a clear career ladder.
- *Your role*—In a larger company, your job is likely to be well-defined. You'll know what is expected of you and where you should be focused.
- *Benefits*—Larger companies sometimes have better benefits (health insurance, dental plans, etc.) because having a large pool of employees puts them in a better bargaining position with insurance companies. You are more likely to find a range of insurance options to choose from.
- *Salaries and bonuses*—Larger companies may be able to offer higher salaries and annual or target-based bonuses because they have more money than smaller companies.
- *Location*—When you work for a larger company, be prepared to be sent where they need you. You could end up anywhere in the country or in the world!
- *Training and educational benefits*—Larger companies often have extensive training programs or pay for most or all of your continuing education credits.
- *Other opportunities*—A larger company may have more types of jobs, meaning that you can move "sideways" into a different type of work, as well as moving up the ladder in your original career track.

SMALL COMPANIES

Small companies have the following pros and cons:

- *Structure*—Smaller companies are often more flexible than larger ones. This means they can respond to changes in the market quickly. When a nimble company pivots, you can pivot with it.
- *Your role*—In a smaller company, your job may grow and change more easily than in a larger company.
- *Benefits*—Smaller companies may offer only one (or no) health insurance option, and may offer fewer benefits than a larger company. However, they are in a better position to be flexible when you have something unexpected come up—and that will depend more on your boss's attitude than on the rules a larger company would have to apply.
- *Salaries and bonuses*—Smaller companies may not be able to offer the highest salaries or bonuses.
- *Location*—When you work for a smaller company, you are most likely to be working where the company is based. That means you have a better chance of staying in your own community, if that's an important factor for you.
- *Training and educational benefits*—Smaller companies don't usually run their own training programs, but they do offer apprenticeships with seasoned workers. Some small companies will pay for training and continuing education at nearby community or technical colleges and trade schools.
- *Other opportunities*—With a smaller company, you have a better opportunity to see how a business is run and to learn about the organizational and management side of the company, which is very useful if you might want to be a boss yourself one day.

Making the Most of Your Experiences

As mentioned earlier, experiences you gain out in the real world are very important pieces of the puzzle that includes your education. In other words, don't just use the time you spend in the classroom learning algebra or calculus, for example, to determine if you have picked the right career path. Getting out in the real world, perhaps working in an office, will help you determine what you do and don't like and what kind of shape you want your career to take. It doesn't hurt your résumé and college applications, either!

It can be hard to get your foot in the door, though. How do you get experience in the real world without having a degree or any experience to begin with? Try these approaches to gaining some much-needed experience:

- Become a math tutor at your high school or local library.
- Volunteer at a charitable or nonprofit organization that you support and ask them for a professional reference moving forward.
- Write a blog in the mathematical area where you want to get experience.
- Become an active contributor on relevant discussion boards.

Be sure to ask for lots of feedback from your mentors, bosses, and others. Don't be afraid to ask for advice, and be sure to have an open attitude about the information you get back.

BUILD YOUR PEOPLE SKILLS

The ability to get along with people is one of three most important factors of a successful career in any field. You'll be interacting with lots of people—clients, coworkers, supervisors, and others. The ability to communicate well—both verbally and in writing—is essential to getting a job, keeping a job, and doing that job well.

There are some basic people skills that anybody can learn—and that are useful for everyone, regardless of their career plans. Let's take a look at some of those important skills.

Relating to Other People

This can be summed up as treating others the way you would want them to treat you. For instance:

- Try to see the other person's point of view (even if it's different from yours). Empathy and compassion go a long way.

- Be understanding and respectful toward other people.
- Be patient—nobody is perfect (including you).
- Pay attention and show genuine interest—everyone has something interesting about them. Take the time to find out what it is!

Communication Skills

Good communication is essential in work and in life. Basic communication skills include the following:

- *Active listening*—Paying attention to what the other person is actually saying and responding to it (not just planning what you're going to say next).
- *Speaking*—Expressing yourself simply and clearly in spoken words.
- *Writing*—Expressing yourself simply, clearly, and with sufficient detail in writing. Avoid a lot of extra words that can confuse the reader, but don't leave out anything important.
- *Body language*—Nonverbal communication is just as important as verbal communication. Pay attention to the messages you're sending with your face, gestures, and posture, and pay attention to the nonverbal messages you're receiving from the people around you.

Character

Your character includes your personality and the choices you make based on your values and beliefs. Important character traits include the following:

- *Honesty and trust*—Honesty and trust form the basis of any relationship, whether personal or professional. This includes trusting others as well as being trustworthy yourself. When you and your coworkers know you can count on each other, you can accomplish anything. When clients know they can trust you and the work you do for them, you will be set up for a lifetime of success.
- *A sense of humor*—Knowing when to use humor to lighten a situation is a great people skill. Used appropriately, humor can defuse tension and conflict, and you will be able and willing to laugh at yourself.

- *Being supportive and helpful*—Offer to do a little more than required or to help someone out when they need it. If someone is having a hard day, be respectful of their feelings.
- *Flexibility*—Be ready to adapt to changing situations, conditions, and workflow.
- *Good judgment*—Choose your own behavior—don't just go along with something if your gut says it's not a good idea.

When you get to chapter 4, you'll learn more about putting your people skills into action to get and keep the job you want.

Networking

Because it's so important, another last word about networking. It's important to develop mentor relationships even at this stage. Remember that up to 85 percent of jobs are found through personal contacts.[2] If you know someone in the field, don't hesitate to reach out. Be patient and polite, but ask for help, perspective, and guidance.

There are basically two kinds of networking:

- *Internal networking*—This involves reaching out to people you already know, such as at your internship or at school. These people don't necessarily have to work in mathematics. They may have other advice or ideas that will help you on your journey. Be sure to give back, too. You don't want to be the one who is always asking for help but never giving any! Take care of these relationships. They are valuable in too many ways to list.
- *External networking*—This involves meeting new people at work, in extracurricular clubs, in student chapters of professional associations, at conferences or workshops, or anywhere that you don't already spend a lot of time. If you discover someone you'd like to know or ask a question, seek them out and introduce yourself. Be polite and professional. Don't take up too much of their time, at least at first.

If you don't know anyone, ask your school guidance counselor to help you make connections. Or pick up the phone yourself. Reaching out with a genuine interest in knowledge and a real curiosity about the field will go a long way.

You don't need a job or an internship just yet—just a connection that could blossom into a mentoring relationship. Follow these important but simple rules for the best results when networking:

- Do your homework about a potential contact, connection, university, school, or employer before you make contact. Be sure to have a general understanding of what they do and why. But don't be a know-it-all. Be open and ready to ask good questions.
- Be considerate of professionals' time and resources. Think about what they can get from you in return for mentoring or helping you.
- Speak and write with proper English. Proofread all your letters, emails, and even texts. Think about how you will be perceived at all times.
- Always stay positive.
- Show your passion for the subject matter.

Here are some places you can start networking:

- *Clubs*—If your school has a mathematics club or team or something similar, join and be an active member. Invite people you'd like to learn from to come and speak to the club or give the club a tour of their workplace.
- *Volunteering and internships*—These activities give you unique opportunities to learn from and get to know experienced professionals.
- *Professional organizations*—Some of these have student chapters or special events that students can attend. See the resources section near the end of the book for a list of professional organizations related to mathematics.
- *Social media*—Some social media sites, such as LinkedIn, let you connect with professional organizations as well as people in the field. However, just as with all social media, be wary of sharing personal information with people you don't know personally, especially while you are a minor.

Tip: Maintain and cultivate professional relationships. Write thank-you notes when professionals take the time to meet with you or share their knowledge and expertise in any form, send updates about your progress and tell them where you decide to go to college, and check in occasionally. If you want to find a good mentor, you need to be a gracious and willing mentee.

Summary

In this chapter, you learned even more about what it's like to work in the mathematics/statistics field. This chapter discussed the educational requirements in general. You also learned about getting experience in the field before you enter college as well as during the educational process. At this time, you should have a good idea of the educational requirements for your area of interest. You hopefully even contemplated some questions about what kind of educational career path fits your strengths, time requirements, and wallet. Are you starting to picture your career plan? If not, that's okay, as there's still time.

Remember that no matter which area you pursue, the methodologies change. You must be up to date on the latest changes and developments and meet the continuing education requirements. The bottom line is that you need to have a lifelong love of learning to succeed in this field.

In chapter 3, we go into a lot more detail about pursuing the best educational path. The chapter covers how to find the best value for your education. The chapter includes discussion about financial aid and scholarships. At the end of chapter 3, you should have a much clearer view of the educational landscape and how and where you fit in.

3

Pursuing the Educational Path

It's important to find a school that fits your needs and budget.
SOLSTOCK/E+/GETTY IMAGES

*W*hen it comes time to start looking at colleges, universities, or postsecondary schools, many high schoolers tend to freeze up at the enormity of the job ahead of them. This chapter will help break down this process for you so it won't seem so daunting.

Yes, finding the right college or learning institution is an important task, and it's a big step toward achieving your career goals and dreams. The last chapter covered the various educational requirements of mathematics, which means you should now be ready to find the right institution of learning. This isn't always just a process of finding the very best school that you can afford and can be accepted into, although that might end up being your path. It should also be about finding the right fit so that you can have the best possible experience during your post–high school years.

So here's the truth of it all—attending postsecondary schooling isn't just about getting a degree. It's about learning how to be an adult, managing your life and your responsibilities, being exposed to new experiences, growing as a person, and otherwise moving toward becoming an adult who contributes to society. College—in whatever form it takes for you—offers you an opportunity to actually become an interesting person with perspective on the world and empathy and consideration for people other than yourself, if you let it.

An important component of how successful college will be for you is finding the right fit, the right school that brings out the best in you and challenges you at different levels. I know, no pressure, right? Just as with finding the right profession, your ultimate goal should be to match your personal interests/goals/personality with the college's goals and perspective. For example, small liberal arts colleges have a much different "feel" and philosophy than Big Ten or PAC-12 state schools. And rest assured that all this advice applies even when you're planning on attending community college or another postsecondary school.

Don't worry, though, in addition to these "soft skills," this chapter does dive into the nitty gritty of finding the best schools, no matter what you want to do. In the fields of math and stats specifically, attending a respected program is important to future success, and we cover that in detail in this chapter.

WHAT IS A GAP YEAR?

Taking a year off between high school and college, often called a *gap year*, is normal, perfectly acceptable, and almost required in many countries around the world, and it is becoming increasingly acceptable in the United States as well. Even Malia Obama, daughter of former president Barack Obama, did it. Because the cost of college has gone up dramatically, it literally pays for you to know going in what you want to study, and a gap year—well spent—can do lots to help you answer that question.

Some great ways to spend your gap year include joining the Peace Corps or AmeriCorps organizations, enrolling in a mountaineering program or other gap-year-style programs, backpacking across Europe or other countries on the cheap (be safe and bring a friend), finding a volunteer organization that furthers a cause you believe in or that complements your career aspirations, joining a Road Scholar program (see www.roadscholar.org), teaching English in another country (see https://www.gooverseas.com/blog/best-countries-for-seniors-to-teach-english-abroad for more information), or working and earning money for college!

Many students will find that they get much more out of college when they have a year to mature and to experience the real world. The American Gap Year Association reports from their alumni surveys that students who take gap years show improved civic engagement, improved college graduation rates, and improved GPAs in college.[1] You can use your gap year to explore and solidify your thoughts and plans about a career in mathematics, as well as add impressive experiences to your college application.

See their website at https://gapyearassociation.org/ for lots of advice and resources if you're considering a potentially life-altering experience.

Finding the College That's Right for You

Before you look into which schools have degrees in mathematics and statistics, it will behoove you to take some time to consider what "type" of school will be best for you. If nothing else, answering questions like the following ones can help you narrow your search and focus on a smaller sampling of choices. Write your answers to these questions down somewhere where you can refer to them often, such as in your Notes app on your phone:

- *Size*—Does the size of the school matter to you? Colleges and universities range from sizes of 500 or fewer students to 25,000 students.
- *Community location*—Would you prefer to be in a rural area, a small town, a suburban area, or a large city? How important is the location of the school in the larger world to you?
- *Distance from home*—Will you live at home to save money? If not, how far away from home do you want/are you willing to go? Phrase this in terms of hours away or miles away.
- *Housing options*—What kind of housing would you prefer? Dorms, off-campus apartments, and private homes are all common options.

- *Student body*: How would you like the student body to "look"? Think about coed versus all-male and all-female settings, as well as diversity of the student body, how many students are part-time versus full-time, and the percentage of commuter students. Who will you likely meet there?
- *Academic environment*—Consider which majors are offered and at which levels of degree. Research the student-faculty ratio. Are the classes taught often by actual professors or more often by the teaching assistants? Find out how many internships the school typically provides to students. Are independent study or study abroad programs available in your area of interest?
- *Financial aid availability/cost*—Does the school provide ample opportunities for scholarships, grants, work-study programs, and the like? Does cost play a role in your options? (For most people, it does.)
- *Support services*—Investigate the strength of the academic and career placement counseling services of the school.
- *Social activities and athletics*—Does the school offer clubs that you are interested in? Which sports are offered? Are scholarships available?
- *Specialized programs*—Does the school offer honors programs or programs for veterans or students with disabilities or special needs?

"What can you do with a math degree? It took me a while to connect math to the job market. What I learned was that studying math helps you to think logically, regardless of what you are doing. You approach the world in this structured way—organized and fact-based. A math degree helps you approach challenges and issues in life in a structured way that helps you solve them."— Sean Fahey, mathematician

Not all of these questions are going to be important to you, and that's fine. Be sure to make note of aspects that don't matter so much to you, too, such as size or location. You might change your mind as you go to visit colleges, but it's important to make note of where you're at to begin with.

CONSIDER THE SCHOOL'S REPUTATION

One factor in choosing a college or certificate program is the school's reputation. This reputation is based on the quality of education previous students have had there. If you go to a school with a healthy reputation in your field, it gives potential employers a place to start when they are considering your credentials and qualifications.

Factors vary depending on which schools offer the program you want, so take these somewhat lightly. Some of the factors affecting reputation generally include these:

- *Nonprofit or for-profit*—In general, schools that are nonprofit (or not-for-profit) organizations have better reputations than for-profit schools. In fact, it's best to avoid for-profit schools. For one, the intensity of academic programs may be reduced to allow students with lower grades and abilities to keep up with courses.
- *Accreditation*—Your program must be accredited by a regional accrediting body to be taken seriously in the professional world. It would be very rare to find an unaccredited college or university with a good reputation.
- *Acceptance rate*—Schools that accept a very high percentage of applicants can have lower reputations than those that accept a smaller percentage. That's because a high acceptance rate can indicate that there isn't much competition for those spaces, or that standards are not as high.
- *Alumni*—What have graduates of the program gone on to do? The college's or department's website can give you an idea of what their graduates are doing.
- *History*—Schools that have been around a long time tend to be doing something right. They also tend to have good alumni networks, which can help you when you're looking for a job or a mentor.
- *Faculty*—Schools with a high percentage of permanent faculty versus adjunct faculty tend to have better reputations. Bear in mind that if you're going to a specialized program or certification program, this might be reversed—these programs are frequently taught by experts who are working in the field.
- *Departments*—A department at one school might have a better reputation than a similar department at a school that's more highly ranked

overall. If the department you'll be attending is well known and respected, that could be more important than the reputation of the institution itself.

There are a lot of websites that claim to have the "Top 10 Schools for Statistics" or "Best 25 Mathematics Programs." It's hard to tell which of those are truly accurate. So where do you begin? *US News & World Report* is a great place to start to find a college or university with a great reputation. Go to www.usnews.com/education to find links to the highest-ranked schools for the undergraduate or graduate degree programs that you're interested in.

GEORGE ECKERT: BIOSTATISTICIAN

George Eckert
COURTESY OF GEORGE ECKERT

George Eckert received his bachelor's in mathematics and statistics (combined degree) at Miami University in Oxford, Ohio. He received his master's degree in Applied Statistics at Ohio State. He has been working as a biostatistician at the Indiana University School of Medicine in the department of biostatistics for 26 years. He is currently a supervisor of the biostatistics staff at the Indiana University School of Medicine.

Can you explain how you became interested in statistics as a career path?
I had always been interested in math, because I was good at it and it seemed like a promising career path. While I was getting my undergraduate degree, a researcher/statistician came to talk about his career and explain what he did. I thought it was really interesting. Therefore, I took statistics classes during my undergraduate degree, and then pursued the master's degree in statistics. At that time, there weren't many biostatistics degrees offered. I took biology classes, too, because I really liked the biostatistics applications specifically. It was much more interesting to me than industry, engineering, etc.

What's a "typical" day in your job?

It varies a lot. There are many different roles. I interact with researchers, helping them plan and design studies, and work directly with researchers. They explain what the results show, and we help them translate the data so people can understand it. I have lots of interaction with others. There is also the actual statistical analysis, of course, including programming and coding, and looking at the data to see if makes sense. I work on a lot of different projects at any one time. There are usually several large projects over a long period of time, combined with small projects that take a few days total.

I like that there is so much variety—I deal with lots of different aspects of medicine. I learn a lot about background information, which is very interesting.

How has the job changed in the last twenty years?

The biggest change is around the technology and the general changes in communication. People expect to have things much faster now, and that isn't realistic.

There are more people involved in research who understand what we are doing and the value we add than ever before. That's positive, obviously. Our role is recognized. Funding sources are often through NIH [National Institutes of Health] or AHA [American Heart Association], for example, and the studies that have strong detail are more likely to get funded—and researchers recognize that we can add that detail.

What's the best part of being in this field?

The variety is great. There is always something to learn. There are new statistics techniques, new programming languages, new medical background of research projects, and so on. It never gets boring!

What's the most challenging part of this field?

Deadlines! Meeting time lines and getting the information you need in time to do a good job can be challenging. You might get the data a month later than you expected but still need to make the date. Researchers and/or funding sources apply pressure due to conference deadlines, etc.

Do you think the current education adequately prepares students to enter the field?

I think so. I am in charge of hiring, and we have not had trouble finding people who are prepared. Each school focuses on different things, both on statistical methods as well as programming languages. We usually hire master's or PhD holders. We don't hire bachelor's degree holders here. Most people have a biostatistics degree, but sometimes they are just statistics degrees. The data science degree is a new one, and we haven't hired from there yet.

Where do you see the field going in the future?

It will continue to be very important, because there is a large amount of data out there being collected. This might be in the form of hospital records, patient information, etc. The statistical methods being used are expanding fairly quickly. How do we analyze that type of data? Methods are improving and changing. Statisticians and computer scientists are working together to use this data. Big data plus biostatistics is the next big thing.

What traits or skills make for a good biostatistician?

Programming skills are important, and you need a good math background, of course. The most important thing that people don't really think of as they go through school are communications skills. You have to talk to researchers and find out what they really want. You need to help them be clear about what they really want from a study. Help them define the study. That is part of our role, to educate them about what can be done with their data. Communication skills are undervalued but really important in this job. You aren't taught communications skills during coursework, but you can and should work on them and hone them over time.

What advice do you have for young people considering a career in statistics?

It's a really good area to work in, and there are lots of jobs. If you're interested in the health care/medicine industry and have strong math and communications skills, it's a great area to work in.

How can a young person prepare for this career while in high school?

Do well in math courses, first off. You need a good math background. Classes in biology and science help, but more of it is having an interest in these areas. If you are interested in the topics, that goes a long way. The application should interest you as well.

Any closing comments?

Working in the university setting is very different than working in industry (such as in pharmaceuticals or device manufacturing)—you can make a lot more money in industry, for one. It all depends on what you are good at and what you enjoy. If you are stronger at programming than communication, industry might be a better setting for you. Regardless, there are a lot of opportunities out there.

After the Research, Trust Your Gut

US News & World Report puts it best when they say the college that fits you best is one that will do all these things:

- Offers a degree that matches your interests and needs
- Provides a style of instruction that matches the way you like to learn
- Provides a level of academic rigor to match your aptitude and preparation
- Offers a community that feels like home to you
- Values you for what you do well

According to the National Center for Education Statistics (NCES), which is part of the US Department of Education, six years after entering college for an undergraduate degree, only 60 percent of students have graduated. Barely half of those students will graduate from college in their lifetime. By the same token, it's never been more important to get your degree. College graduates with a bachelor's degree typically earn 66 percent more than those with only a high school diploma; and are also far less likely to face unemployment. Also, over the course of a lifetime, the average worker with a bachelor's degree will earn approximately $1 million more than a worker without a postsecondary education.

As you look at the facts and figures, you also need to think about a less-quantifiable aspect of choosing a college or university: *fit.* What does that mean? It's hard to describe, but students know it when they feel it. It means finding the school that not only offers the program you want, but also the school that feels right. Many students have no idea what they're looking for in a school until they walk onto the campus for a visit. Suddenly, they'll say to themselves "This is the one!"

While you're evaluating a particular institution's offerings with your conscious mind, your unconscious mind is also at work, gathering information about all kinds of things at lightning speed. When it tells your conscious mind what it's decided, we call that a "gut reaction." Pay attention to your gut reactions! There's good information in there.

Touring the campus and talking to current students are important steps in getting a realistic impression of the school.
SDI PRODUCTIONS/ISTOCK/GETTY IMAGES

Hopefully, this section has impressed upon you the importance of finding the right college fit. Take some time to paint a mental picture about the kind of university or school setting that will best meet your needs.

> *Note:* According to the US Department of Education, as many as 32 percent of college students transfer colleges during the course of their educational career. This is to say that the decision you initially make is not set in stone. Do your best to make a good choice, but remember that you can change your mind, your major, and even your campus. Many students do it and go on to have great experiences and earn great degrees.

HONING YOUR DEGREE PLAN

This section outlines the different approaches you can take to get a degree that will land you your dream job in mathematics, whether it be as a statistician, professor, actuary, economist, or something related to all of these.

RELEVANT DEGREE PATHS TO CONSIDER

As you've no doubt learned if you've read this far into the book, the mathematics umbrella has many varied, but related, professions within it. No matter which area you want to focus on, having at least a bachelor's degree (a four-year degree) is required, and advanced degrees (master's degrees and PhDs) are even more common and desirable in this profession. Consider these points:

- Since a bachelor's degree is a four-year process, it's cheaper and takes less time than a master's or PhD. It *is* possible to start a career in mathematics/statistics with a bachelor's degree, although your employment opportunities and salary will be more limited. The federal government is a common hirer of bachelor's degrees holders in math and stats, for example. Other common roles include accountants, bookkeepers, and logisticians. Once you are hired, you may be in a position to have your employer pay for you to get your advanced degree while you work for them.
- If you want to enter the workforce as an economist, biostatistician, actuary, or financial analyst, you'll likely need a master's degree (a six-year degree).
- Some positions in mathematics require PhDs (usually an eight-year process), including college professors and advanced academic research and statistics positions. If you don't plan on working in academia in some manner, pursuing a PhD might not be worth it.
- Many, if not most, good math PhD programs in the United States allow you to leave after a couple of years with a master's. If you can get into a good PhD program, you can start it and reevaluate your options after two years. Of course, you would want to verify that they offer a master's, just in case.

So, what does the typical mathematics degree require of you? Well, as a sampling, the typical student will be required to take at least some of the following classes before moving into specifics related to their area of choice:

- Algebra, combinatorics, and number theory
- Multiple calculus classes
- Mathematical analysis, including vector and real analysis
- Applied mathematics, including statistics and probability
- Mathematical logic and reasoning, including set theory

In addition to the foundational mathematics classes, students studying to be statisticians also take classes similar to these:

- Mathematical statistics
- Specialized statistics topics, such as regression, time series, actuarial studies, biostatistics, and statistical computing
- Data, inference, and decisions
- Sampling surveys
- Reproducible statistical data science

These are just samples of what you will take to gain your degree. Be sure to check the curricula of the schools you're considering attending for more specific information.

Starting Your College Search

If you're currently in high school and you are serious about working in the field of math or stats, start by finding three to five schools in a realistic location (for you) that offer the degree in question. Not every school near you or that you have an initial interest in will probably offer the degree you desire, so narrow your choices accordingly. With that said, consider attending a public university in your resident state, if possible, which will save you lots of money. Private institutions don't typically discount resident student tuition costs.

Be sure you research the basic GPA and SAT or ACT requirements of each school as well.

Tip: For those of you applying to associate's degree programs or greater, most advisers recommend that students take both the ACT and the SAT tests during their junior year (spring at the latest). (The ACT test is generally considered more weighted in science, so take that into consideration.) You can retake these tests and use your highest score, so be sure to leave time to retake early senior year if needed. You want your best score to be available to all the schools you're applying to by January 1 of your senior year, which will also enable them to be considered with any scholarship applications. (Unless you want to do *early decision*, which can provide you certain benefits.) Keep in mind these are general time lines—be sure to check the exact deadlines and calendars of the schools to which you're applying! See the section entitled "Know the Deadlines" for more information about various deadlines.

Once you have found four to five schools in a realistic location for you that offer the degree you want to pursue, spend some time on their websites studying the requirements for admissions. Most universities will list the average stats for the last class accepted to the program. Important factors weighing on your decision of what schools to apply to should include whether or not you meet the requirements, your chances of getting in (but shoot high!), tuition costs, and availability of scholarships and grants, location, and the school's reputation and licensure/graduation rates.

The order of these characteristics will depend on your grades and test scores, your financial resources, and other personal factors. You of course want to find a university with a strong math department, and one that also matches your academic rigor and practical needs.

APPLYING AND GETTING ADMITTED

Once you've narrowed down your list of potential schools, of course you'll want to be accepted. First, you need to apply.

There isn't enough room in this book to include everything you need to know about applying to colleges. But here is some useful information to get you started. Remember, every college and university is unique, so be sure to be in touch with their admissions offices so you don't miss any special requirements or deadlines.

It's a good idea to make yourself a "to do" list while you're a junior in high school. Already a senior? Already graduated? No problem. It's never too late to start.

Before you go to college, you have to be admitted.

MAKE THE MOST OF SCHOOL VISITS

If it's at all practical and feasible, you should visit the schools you're considering. To get a real feel for any college or school, you need to walk around the campus and buildings, spend some time in the common areas where students hang out, and sit in on a few classes. You can also sign up for campus tours, which are typically given by current students. This is another good way to see the school and ask questions of someone who knows. Be sure to visit the specific school/building that covers your possible major as well. The website and brochures won't be able to convey that intangible feeling you'll get from a visit.

In addition to the questions listed in the previous section in this chapter entitled "Finding the College That's Right for You," consider these questions as well. Make a list of questions that are important to you before you visit.

- What is the makeup of the current freshman class? Is the campus diverse?
- What is the meal plan like? What are the food options?
- Where do most of the students hang out between classes? (Be sure to visit this area.)
- How long does it take to walk from one end of the campus to the other?
- What types of transportation are available for students? Does campus security provide escorts to cars, dorms, and so forth, at night?

In order to be ready for your visit and make the most of it, consider these tips and words of advice.

Before you go, do the following:

- Be sure to do some research. At the least, spend some time on the college website. Make sure your questions aren't addressed adequately there first.
- Make a list of questions.
- Arrange to meet with a professor in your area of interest or to visit the specific school.
- Be prepared to answer questions about yourself and why you are interested in this school.
- Dress in neat, clean, and casual clothes. Avoid overly wrinkled clothing or anything with stains.
- Listen and take notes.
- Don't interrupt.
- Be positive and energetic.
- Make eye contact when someone speaks directly to you.
- Ask questions.
- Thank people for their time
- Finally, be sure to send thank-you notes or emails after the visit is over. Remind the recipient when you visited the campus and thank them for their time.

STANDARDIZED TESTS

Many colleges and universities require scores from standardized tests that are supposed to measure your readiness for college and ability to succeed. There is debate about how accurate these tests are, so some institutions don't ask for them anymore. But most do, so you should expect to take them.

Undergraduate Level Tests

To apply to an undergraduate program, students generally take either the SAT or the ACT. Both cover reading, writing, and math. Both have optional essays. Both are accepted by colleges and universities. Both take nearly the same amount of time to complete. If one test is preferred over another by schools, it's usually more about where you live than about the test.

- *SAT*—Offered by the CollegeBoard.org. There are twenty SAT subject tests that you can take to show knowledge of special areas, such as math 1 and math 2, biology (ecological or molecular), chemistry, physics, as well as US or world history and numerous languages.
- *ACT*—Offered by ACT.org. There aren't any subject tests available with the ACT. Questions are a little easier on the ACT, but you don't have as much time to answer them.

Ultimately, which test you take comes down to personal preference. Many students choose to take both exams.

Graduate Level Tests

- *GRE* (Graduate Record Exam)—The GRE is published by ETS (Educational Testing Service). The GRE is the most widely used admission test for graduate and professional schools. It covers verbal and quantitative reasoning and analytical writing. The test results are considered along with your undergraduate record for admissions decisions to most graduate programs.
- *GRE subject tests*—Some graduate programs also want to see scores from subject tests. GRE subject tests are offered in biology, chemistry, literature in English, mathematics, physics, and psychology. The GRE subject test in mathematics is designed to assess a candidate's potential for graduate or postgraduate study in the field of mathematics.

- *MCAT (Medical College Admission Test)*—The MCAT is administered by the Association of American Medical Colleges (AAMC). MCAT is the standardized test for admission to medical school programs in allopathic, osteopathic, podiatric, or veterinary medicine (some veterinary programs accept the GRE instead).
- *LSAT (Law School Admission Test)*—The LSAT is administered by the Law School Admission Council seven times a year. This test for prospective law school candidates is the only test accepted for admission purposes by all ABA-accredited law schools and Canadian common-law law schools.

KNOW THE DEADLINES

- *Early decision (ED)* deadlines are usually in November, with acceptance decisions announced in December. Note that if you apply for ED admission and are accepted, that decision is usually binding, so only apply ED if you know exactly which school you want to go to and are ready to commit.
- *ED II* is a second round of early decision admissions. Not every school that does ED will also have an ED II. For those that do, deadlines are usually in January with decisions announced in February.
- *Regular decision* deadlines can be as early as January 1 but can go later. Decision announcements usually come out between mid-March and early April.
- *Rolling admission* is used by some schools. Applications are accepted at any time, and decisions are announced on a regular schedule. Once the incoming class is full, admissions for that year will close.

THE COMMON APP

The Common Application form is a single, detailed application form that is accepted by more than 900 colleges and universities in the United States. Instead of filling out a different application form for every school you want to apply to, you fill out one form and have it sent to all the schools you're interested in. The Common App itself is free, and most schools don't charge for submitting it.

If you don't want to use the Common App for some reason, most colleges will also let you apply with a form on their website. There are a few institutions that only want you to apply through their sites and other highly regarded institutions that only accept the Common App. Be sure you know what the schools you're interested in prefer.

The Common App's website (www.commonapp.org) has a lot of useful information, including tips for first-time applicants and for transfer students.

ESSAYS

Part of any college application is a written essay, sometimes even two or three. Some colleges provide writing prompts they want you to address. The Common App has numerous prompts that you can choose from. Here are some issues to consider when writing your essays:

- *Topic*—Choose something that has some meaning for you and that you can speak about in a personal way. This is your chance to show the college or university who you are as an individual. It doesn't have to be about an achievement or success, and it shouldn't be your whole life story. Maybe write about a topic that relates to a time you learned something or had an insight into yourself.
- *Timing*—Start working on your essays the summer before senior year, if possible. You won't have a lot of other homework in your way, and you'll have time to prepare thoughtful comments and polish your final essay.
- *Length*—Aim for between 250 and 650 words. The Common App leans toward the long end of that range, while individual colleges might lean toward the shorter end.
- *Writing*—Use straightforward language. Don't turn in your first draft—work on your essay, improving it as you go. Ask someone else to read it and tell you what they think. Ask your English teacher to look at it and make suggestions. Do *not* let someone else write any portion of your essay. It needs to be *your* ideas and your writing in order to represent *you*.
- *Proofing*—Make sure your essay doesn't have any obvious errors. Run spellcheck, but don't trust it to find everything (spellcheckers are notorious for introducing weird errors). Have someone you trust read it over for you and note spelling, grammar, and other mistakes. Nobody

can proofread their own work and find every mistake—what you'll see is what you expect to see. Even professional editors need other people to proofread their writing! Don't be embarrassed to ask for help.

LETTERS OF RECOMMENDATION

Most college applications ask for letters of recommendation from people who know you well and can speak to what you're like as a student and as a person. How many you need varies from school to school, so check with the admissions office website to see what they want. Some schools don't want any!

Who Should You Ask for a Letter?

Some schools will tell you pretty specifically whom they want to hear from. Others leave it up to you. Choose people who know you and think well of you. Here are some examples:

- One or two teachers of your best academic subjects (math, science, social studies, etc.)
- Teacher of your best elective subject (art, music, media, etc.)
- Adviser for a club that you are active in
- School counselor
- School principal (but only if you've taken a class with them or they know you individually as a student)
- Community member you've worked with, such as a scout leader, volunteer group leader, or religious leader
- Boss at a job you've held

When Should You Ask for a Letter?

Don't wait until applications are due. Give people plenty of time to prepare a good recommendation letter for you. If possible, ask for these letters in late spring or early summer of your junior year.

Submitting Your Letters of Recommendation

Technically, you're not supposed to read your recommendation letters. That lets recommenders speak more freely about you. Some might show you the letter anyway, but that's up to them. Don't ask to see it!

Recommenders can submit their letters electronically either directly to the institutions you're applying to or through the Common App. Your job is to be sure they know the submission deadlines well in advance so they can send in the letters on time.

ADMISSIONS REQUIREMENTS

Each college or university will have their own admissions requirements. In addition, the specific program or major you want to go into may have admissions requirements of their own, in addition to the institution's requirements.

It's your responsibility to go to each institution's website and be sure you know and understand their requirements. That includes checking out each department site, too, to find any special prerequisites or other things that they're looking for.

THE MOST PERSONAL OF PERSONAL STATEMENTS

The personal statement you include with your application to college is extremely important, especially when your GPA and SAT/ACT scores are on the border of what is typically accepted. Write something that is thoughtful and conveys your understanding of the profession, as well as your desire to work in the world of mathematics/statistics. Why are you uniquely qualified? Why are you a good fit for this university and program or these types of students? These essays should be highly personal (the "personal" in personal statement). Will the admissions professionals who read it, along with hundreds of others, come away with a snapshot of who you really are and what you are passionate about?

Look online for some examples of good ones, which will give you a feel for what works. Be sure to check your specific school for length guidelines, format requirements, and any other guidelines they expect you to follow. Most important, make sure your passion for your potential career comes through—although make sure it is also genuine.

And of course, be sure to proofread it several times and ask a professional (such as your school writing center or your local library services) to proofread it as well.

What's It Going to Cost You?

So, the bottom line—what will your education end up costing you? Of course that depends on many factors, including the type and length of degree, where you attend (in-state or not, private or public institution), how much in scholarships or financial aid you're able to obtain, your family or personal income, and many other factors.

> "College may seem expensive. But the truth is that most students pay less than their college's sticker price, or published price, thanks to financial aid. So instead of looking at the published price, concentrate on your net price—the real price you'll pay for a college. . . . Your net price is a college's sticker price for tuition and fees minus the grants, scholarships, and education tax benefits you receive. The net price you pay for a particular college is specific to you because it's based on your personal circumstances and the college's financial aid policies."—BigFuture

The College Entrance Examination Board (see www.collegeboard.org) tracks and summarizes financial data from colleges and universities all over the United States. A sample of data from the 2019–2020 academic year is shown in tables 3.1 and 3.2.

Table 3.1.   Average Estimated Annual Costs by Degree Type, 2019–2020

Sector	Undergraduate degree total (tuition, fees, room, and board)	Master's degree total (tuition, fees, room, and board)	Doctoral degree total (tuition, fees, room, and board)	Average percent increase in one year
Private nonprofit four-year	$48,380	$43,380	$60,160	3.3%
Public four-year	$19,460	$19,570	$23,370	2.7%

Sources: College Board, Annual Survey of Colleges; NCES, IPEDS Fall 2019 enrollment data and IPEDS 2018 Institutional Characteristics data.

Notes: Other expense categories, such as books, supplies, and transportation, are not included here.

Table 3.2.   Average Estimated Annual Costs by Sector, 2019–2020

Sector	Tuition and fees	Room and board	Total	Average percent increase in one year
Private nonprofit four-year	$36,880	$12,990	$49,870	3.4%
Public four-year out-of-state	$26,820	$11,510	$38,330	2.4%
Public four-year in-state	$10,440	$11,510	$21,950	2.3%
Public two-year in-district	$3,730	$8,990	$12,720	2.8%

Sources: College Board, Annual Survey of Colleges; NCES, IPEDS Fall 2019 enrollment data and IPEDS 2018 Institutional Characteristics data.

Notes: Other expense categories, such as books, supplies, and transportation, are not included here.

Table 3.1 shows the average estimated annual costs depending on the degree level you are pursuing. Table 3.2 shows undergraduate costs depending on the type of university. In both cases, costs shown are for one year.

Keep in mind these are averages and reflect the *published* prices, not the net prices. As an example of net cost, in 2019–2020, full-time, in-state students at public four-year colleges must cover an average of about $15,400 in tuition and fees and room and board after grant aid and tax benefits, in addition to paying for books and supplies and other living expenses.

If you read more specific data about a particular university or find averages in your particular area of interest, you should assume those numbers are closer to reality than these averages, as they are more specific. This data helps to show you the ballpark figures.

Generally speaking, there is about a 3 percent annual increase in tuition and associated costs to attend college. In other words, if you are expecting to attend college two years after this data was collected, you need to add approximately 6 percent to these numbers. Keep in mind again that this assumes no financial aid or scholarships of any kind (so it's not the net cost).

This chapter also covers finding the most affordable path to get the degree you want. Later in this section, you'll also learn how to prime the pumps and get as much money for college as you can.

FINANCIAL AID AND STUDENT LOANS

Finding the money to attend college, whether for two or four years, an online program, or a vocational career college, can seem overwhelming. But you can do it if you have a plan before you actually start applying to college.

NOT ALL FINANCIAL AID IS CREATED EQUAL

Educational institutions tend to define financial aid as any scholarship, grant, loan, or paid employment that assists students to pay their college expenses. Notice that "financial aid" covers both *money you have to pay back* and *money you don't have to pay back.* That's a big difference!

Do Not Have to Be Repaid

- Scholarships
- Grants
- Work-Study

Have to Be Repaid *with Interest*

- Federal government loans
- Private loans
- Institutional loans

If you get into your top-choice university, don't let the sticker cost turn you away. Financial aid can come from many different sources, and it's available to cover all different kinds of costs you'll encounter during your years in college, including tuition, fees, books, housing, and food.

Paying for college can take a creative mix of grants, scholarships, and loans, but you can find your way with some help!
ZIMMYTWS/ISTOCK/GETTY IMAGES

The good news is that universities more often offer incentive or tuition discount aid to encourage students to attend. The market is often more competitive in favor of the student and colleges and universities are responding by offering more generous aid packages to a wider range of students than they used to. Here are some basic tips and pointers about the financial aid process:

- You apply for financial aid during your senior year. You must fill out the FAFSA (Free Application for Federal Student Aid) form, which can be filed starting October 1 of your senior year until June of the year you graduate. Because the amount of available aid is limited, it's best to apply as soon as you possibly can. (See fafsa.gov to get started.)
- Be sure to compare and contrast deals you get at different schools. There is room to negotiate with universities. The first offer for aid may not be the best you'll get.
- Wait until you receive all offers from your top schools and then use this information to negotiate with your top choice to see if they will match or beat the best aid package you received.
- To be eligible to keep and maintain your financial aid package, you must meet certain grade/GPA requirements. Be sure you are very clear on these academic expectations and keep up with them.
- You must reapply for federal aid every year.

Tip: Watch out for scholarship scams! You should never be asked to pay to submit the FAFSA form ("free" is in its name) or be required to pay a lot to find appropriate aid and scholarships. These are free services. If an organization promises you you'll get aid or that you have to "act now or miss out," these are both warning signs of a less-reputable organization.

Also, be careful with your personal information to avoid identity theft as well. Simple things like closing and exiting your browser after visiting sites where you entered personal information (like fafsa.gov) goes a long way. Don't share your student aid ID number with anyone, either.

It's important to understand the different forms of financial aid that are available to you. That way, you'll know how to apply for different kinds and get the best financial aid package that fits your needs and strengths. The two main categories that financial aid falls under is *gift aid*, which doesn't have to be repaid, and *self-help aid*, which is either loans that must be repaid or work-study funds that are earned. The next sections cover the various types of financial aid that fit in one of these areas.

GRANTS

Grants typically are awarded to students who have financial needs, but can also be used in the areas of athletics, academics, demographics, veteran support, and special talents. They do not have to be paid back. Grants can come from federal agencies, state agencies, specific universities, and private organizations. Most federal and state grants are based on financial need. Examples of grants are the Pell Grant and the SMART Grant.

SCHOLARSHIPS

Scholarships are merit-based aid that does not have to be paid back. They are typically awarded based on academic excellence or some other special talent, such a music or art. Scholarships also fall under the areas of athletic-based, minority-based, aid for women, and so forth. These are typically not awarded by federal or state governments, but instead come from the specific school you applied to as well as private and nonprofit organizations.

Be sure to reach out directly to the financial aid officers of the schools you want to attend. These people are great contacts that can lead you to many more sources of scholarships and financial aid. (Visit http://www.gocollege.com /financial-aid/scholarships/types/ for lots more information about how scholarships in general work.)

LOANS

Many types of loans are available especially to students to pay for their post-secondary education. However, the important thing to remember here is that loans *must be paid back, with interest.* Be sure you understand the interest rate you will be charged. This is the extra cost of borrowing the money and is usually a percentage of the amount you borrow. Is this fixed or will it change over time? Is the loan and interest deferred until you graduate (meaning you don't have to begin paying it off until after you graduate)? Is the loan subsidized (meaning the federal government pays the interest until you graduate)? These are all points you need to be clear about before you sign on the dotted line.

There are many types of loans offered to students, including need-based loans, non-need-based loans, state loans, and private loans. Two very reputable federal loans are the Perkins Loan and the Direct Stafford Loan. (For more information about student loans, start at https://bigfuture.collegeboard.org /pay-for-college/loans/types-of-college-loans.)

FEDERAL WORK-STUDY

The US federal work-study program provides part-time jobs for undergraduate and graduate students with financial need so they can earn money to pay for educational expenses. The focus of such work is on community service work and work related to a student's course of study. Not all schools participate in this program, so be sure to check with the school financial aid office if this is something you are counting on. The sooner you apply, the more likely you will get the job you desire and be able to benefit from the program, as funds are limited. (See https://studentaid.ed.gov/sa/types/work-study for more information about this opportunity.)

FINANCIAL AID TIPS

- Some colleges/universities will offer tuition discounts to encourage students to attend—so tuition costs can be lower than they look at first.
- Apply for financial aid during your senior year of high school. The sooner you apply, the better your chances.
- Compare offers from different schools—one school may be able to match or improve on another school's financial aid offer.
- Keep your grades up—a good GPA helps a lot when it comes to merit scholarships and grants.
- You have to reapply for financial aid every year, so you'll be filling out that FAFSA form again!
- Look for ways that loans might be deferred or forgiven—service commitment programs are a way to use service to pay back loans.

While You're in College

Once you're in an undergrad program, of course you'll take all the classes required by your major. This will be time consuming and a lot of hard work, as it should be. But there's more to your college experience than that!

One of the great advantages of college is that it's so much more than just training for a particular career. It's your opportunity to become a broader, deeper person. Use your electives to take courses far outside your major. Join clubs, intramural teams, improv groups—whatever catches your interest. Take a foreign language. The broader your worldview is, the more interesting you are as a person, and the more appealing you are to employers in the future!

> "It has always seemed strange to me that in our endless discussions about education so little stress is laid on the pleasure of becoming an educated person, the enormous interest it adds to life. To be able to be caught up into the world of thought—that is to be educated."—Edith Hamilton[2]

WORKING WHILE YOU LEARN

Your classes won't always convey what it's like to do the work in real life. If you have the opportunity, consider some of these ways to learn and work at the same time.

Cooperative Education Programs

Cooperative education (co-op) programs are a structured way to alternate classroom instruction with on-the-job experience. There are co-op programs for all kinds of jobs. Co-op programs are run by the educational institution in partnership with several employers. Students usually alternate semesters in school with semesters at work.

A co-op program is not an internship. Students in co-op jobs typically work forty hours a week during their work semesters and are paid a regular salary. Participating in a co-op program means it will take longer to graduate, but you come out of school with a lot of legitimate work experience.

Be sure the college you attend is truly committed to its co-op program. Some are deeply committed to the idea of co-ops as integral to education, but others treat it more like an add-on program. Also, the company you co-op with is not obliged to hire you at the end of the program. But they can still be an excellent source of good references for you in your job search.

Internships

Internships are another way to gain work experience while you're in school. Internships are offered by employers and usually last one semester or one summer. You might work part-time or full-time, but you're usually paid in experience and college credit rather than money. There are paid internships in some fields, but they aren't common.

Making High School Count

If you are still in high school or middle school, there are many things you can do now to nurture your interest in mathematics and statistics and set yourself up for success. Consider these tips for your remaining years:

- Work on listening well and speaking and communicating clearly. Work on writing clearly and effectively.
- Learn how to learn. This means keeping an open mind, asking questions, asking for help when you need it, taking good notes, and doing your homework.
- Plan a daily homework schedule and keep up with it. Have a consistent, quiet place to study.
- Talk about your career interests with friends, family, and counselors. They may have connections to people in your community who you can shadow or will mentor you.
- Try new interests or activities, especially during your first two years of high school.
- Be involved in extracurricular activities that truly interest you and say something about who you are and want to be.

Kids are under so much pressure these days to "do it all," but you should think about working smarter rather than harder. If you are involved in things you enjoy, your educational load won't seem like such a burden. Be sure to take time for self-care, such as sleep, unscheduled downtime, and other activities that you find fun and energizing. (See chapter 4 for more ways to relieve and avoid stress.)

Remember to take care of yourself and to enjoy the journey to adulthood!
ANTONIOGUILLEM/ISTOCK/GETTY IMAGES

Summary

This chapter dove right in and talked about all the aspects of college and postsecondary schooling that you'll want to consider as you move forward. Remember that finding the right fit is especially important, as it increases the chances that you'll stay in school and finish your degree or program, as well as have an amazing experience while you're there.

In this chapter, you learned a little about what a typical mathematics and statistics degree will require of you. You also learned about how to get the best education for the best deal. You learned a little about scholarships and financial aid, how the SAT and ACT tests work, how to write a unique personal statement that eloquently expresses your passions, and how to do your best at essays and other application requirements.

Use this chapter as a jumping-off point to dig deeper into your particular area of interest. Some tidbits of wisdom to leave you with:

- If you need to, take the SAT and ACT tests early in your junior year so you have time to take them again. Most schools automatically accept the highest scores (but be sure to check your specific schools' policies).
- Don't underestimate how important school visits are, especially in the pursuit of finding the right academic fit. Come prepared to ask questions not addressed on the school website or in the literature.
- Your personal statements/essays are very important pieces of your application that can set you apart from others. Take the time and energy needed to make them unique and compelling.
- Don't assume you can't afford a school based on the "sticker price." Many schools offer great scholarships and aid to qualified students. It doesn't hurt to apply. This advice especially applies to minorities, veterans, and students with disabilities.
- Don't lose sight of the fact that it's important pursue a career that you enjoy, are good at, and are passionate about! You'll be a happier person if you do so.

At this point, your career goals and aspirations should be gelling. At the least, you should have a plan for finding out more information. And don't forget about networking, which was covered in more detail in chapter 2. Remember to do the research about the school or degree program before you reach out and especially before you visit. Faculty and staff find students who ask challenging questions much more impressive than those who ask questions that can be answered by spending ten minutes on the school website.

In chapter 4, we go into detail about the next steps—writing a résumé and cover letter, interviewing well, follow-up communications, and more. This is information you can use to secure internships, volunteer positions, summer jobs, and more. It's not just for college grads. In fact, the sooner you can hone these communication skills, the better off you'll be in the professional world, regardless of your job.

4

Writing Your Résumé and Interviewing

*N*o matter which career you aspire to work in, having a well-written résumé and impeccable interviewing skills will help you reach your ultimate goals. This chapter provides some helpful tips and advice to build the best résumé and cover letter, how to interview well with all your prospective employers, and how to communicate effectively and professionally at all times. All the advice in this chapter isn't just for people entering the workforce full-time, either. It can help you score that internship or summer job or help you give a great college interview to impress the admissions office.

After we talk about writing your résumé, the chapter discusses important interviewing skills that you can build and develop over time. The chapter also has some tips for using social media to your benefit, as well as how to deal successfully with stress, which is an inevitable by-product of a busy life. Let's dive in!

Writing Your Résumé

If you're a teen writing a résumé for your first job, you likely don't have a lot of work experience under your belt yet. Because of this limited work experience, you need to include classes and coursework that are related to the job you're seeking, as well as any school activities and volunteer experience you have. While you are writing your résumé, you might discover some talents and recall some activities you did that you forgot about, which are still important to add. Think about volunteer work, side jobs you've held (tutoring, etc.), and the like. A good approach at this point in your career is to build a functional-type résumé, which focuses on your abilities rather than work experience, and it's discussed in detail next.

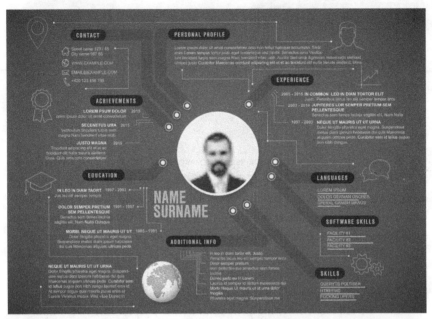

Just because you're in an analytical field doesn't mean your résumé has to be boring looking. Just make sure it's functional and easy to read as well.
ORSONSURF/ISTOCK/GETTY IMAGES

PARTS OF A RÉSUMÉ

As mentioned, the functional résumé is the best approach when you don't have a lot of pertinent work experience, as it is written to highlight your abilities rather than the experience. The other, perhaps more common type of résumé is called the chronological résumé, and it lists a person's accomplishments in reverse chronological order, most recent jobs listed first. This section breaks down and discusses the functional résumé in greater detail.

Here are the essential parts of your resume, listed from the top down:

- *Heading*—This should include your name, address, and contact information, including phone, email, and website if you have one. This information is typically centered on the page.
- *Objective*—This is one sentence that tells that specific employer what kind of position you are seeking. These should be modified to be specific to each potential employer.

- *Education*—Always list your most recent school or program first. Include date of completion (or expected date of graduation), degree or certificate earned, and the institution's name and address. Include workshops, seminars, and related classes here as well.
- *Skills*—Skills include computer literacy, leadership skills, organizational skills, or time-management skills. Be specific in this area when possible and tie your skills to mathematics/statistics when it's appropriate.
- *Activities*—These can be related to skills. Perhaps an activity listed here led to you developing a skill listed above. This section can be combined with the skills section, but it's often helpful to break these apart if you have enough substantive things to say in both areas. Examples include camps, sports teams, leadership roles, community service work, clubs, and organizations, as well as any time you tutored or worked with math or stats.
- *Experience*—If you don't have any actual work experience that's relevant, you might consider skipping this section. However, you can list summer, part-time, and volunteer jobs you've held, again focusing on work related to mathematics.
- *Interests*—This section is optional, but it's a chance to include special talents and interests. Keep it short, factual, and specific.
- *References*—It's best to say that references are available on request. If you do list actual contacts, list no more than three and make sure you inform your contacts that they might be contacted.

The skills, interests, and experience entries can be creatively combined or developed to maximize your abilities and experience. These are not set-in-stone sections that every résumé must have.

"Job security [as a statistician] is excellent. The job market is strong. When you go on job interviews, ask questions about the work environment. Are they going to value what you do and your contributions? Will you be supported when you ask questions? Those things will affect your job satisfaction."—Helena Hoen, biostatistician

If you're still not seeing the big picture here, it's helpful to look at student and part-time résumé examples online to see how others have approached this process. Search for "functional résumé examples" to get a look at some examples.

Even just helping fellow students with math problems can be a good thing to mention as experience.
SDI PRODUCTIONS/E+/GETTY IMAGES

RÉSUMÉ-WRITING TIPS

Regardless of your situation and why you're writing the résumé, there are some basic tips and techniques you should use:

- Keep it short and simple. This includes using a simple, standard font and format. Using one of the résumé templates provided by your word processor software can be a great way to start.
- Use simple language. Keep it to one page.
- Highlight your academic achievements, such as a high GPA (above 3.5) or academic awards. If you have taken classes related to the job you're interviewing for, list those briefly as well.
- Emphasize your extracurricular activities, internships, and so forth. These could include camps, clubs, sports, tutoring, or volunteer work. Use these activities to show your skills, interests, and abilities.

- Use action verbs, such as *led, created, taught, ran, and developed.*
- Be specific and give examples.
- Always be honest.
- Include leadership roles and experience.
- Edit and proofread at least twice and have someone else do the same. Ask a professional (such as your school writing center or your local library services) to proofread it for you also. Don't forget to run spell-check.
- Include a cover letter if necessary (discussed next).

THE COVER LETTER/EMAIL INTRO LETTER

Every résumé you send out through the standard mail should include a cover letter. If you are sending your résumé via email or another electronic format, be sure to provide introductory text that takes the place of the traditional cover letter. This can be the most important part of your job search because it's often the first thing that potential employers read. By including this, you're showing the employers that you took the time to learn about their organization and address them personally. This goes a long way to show that you're interested in the position.

Be sure to call the company or verify on the website the name and title of the person to whom you should address the letter/email. This letter/email should be brief. Introduce yourself and begin with a statement that will grab the person's attention. Keep in mind that they will potentially be receiving hundreds of résumé and cover letters for an open position.

As with the résumé, you have a little room to be creative, but the cover letter should contain the following parts in order from top to bottom:

- Your name, address, phone number, email address
- Today's date
- The recipient's name, title, company name, and company address
- Salutation
- Body (usually one to three paragraphs)
- Closing (your signature and name)

An email would not include the address or date. The body portion should mention how you heard about the position, something extra about you that will interest the potential employer, practical skills you can bring to the position, and past experience related to the job. You should apply the facts outlined in your résumé to the job to which you're applying.

Your cover letter/email should be as short as possible while still conveying a sense of who you are and why you want this particular job or to work for this particular company. Do your research into the company and include some details about the company in your letter/email—this demonstrates that you cared enough to take the time to learn something about them.

Note: Always try to find out the name and title of the person who will be handling your application. This is usually listed in the job posting, but if not, taking the time to track it down yourself on the company website can pay off. Think about it. Imagine that you read nine cover letters address to "Dear sir or madam" and then you get a tenth addressed to you using your name. Wouldn't that one catch your attention?

Here are a few more things to keep in mind when writing your cover letter/email:

- As with the résumé, proofread it many times and have others proofread it, too. You don't want your potential employer to discard a great letter you worked so hard on just because you forgot to finish a sentence or made some clumsy mistake.
- Use "Mr." for male names and "Ms." for female names in your salutation. If you can't figure out the sex of the person who will be handling your application from their name, just use their full name ("Dear Jamie Smith").
- As much as possible, connect the specific qualifications the company is looking for with your skill set and experience. The closer you can make yourself resemble the ideal candidate described in the ad, the more likely they will call you for an interview.
- If you're lacking one or more qualifications the employer is looking for, just ignore it. Don't call attention to it by pointing it out or making an excuse. Leave it up to them to decide how important it is and whether they still want to call you in for an interview. Your other skills and experience may more than make up for any one lack.

- You want to seem eager, competent, helpful, and dependable. Think about things from the employer's point of view. Focus your letter much more on what *you* can do for *them* than on what they can do for you. Be someone that *you* would want to hire.
- For more advice on cover letters, check out the free guide by Résumé Genius at https://resumegenius.com/cover-letters-the-how-to-guide.

RÉSUMÉS, COVER LETTERS, AND ONLINE JOB APPLICATIONS

Résumés and cover letters are holdovers from the era before the Internet—from before personal computers, even. They were designed to be typed on paper and delivered through the mail. Obviously, nowadays much of the job application process has moved online. Nevertheless, the essential concepts communicated by the résumé and cover letter haven't changed. Most employers who accept online applications either ask that you email or upload your résumé.

Those who ask you to email your résumé will specify which document formats they accept. The Adobe Acrobat PDF is often preferred, because many programs can display a PDF (including web browsers), and documents in this format are mostly uneditable—that is, they can't easily be changed. Most word processing programs have an option under the save command that allows you to save your work as a PDF.

In these cases, you attach the résumé to your email, and your email itself becomes the "cover letter." The same principles of the cover letter discussed in this section apply to this email, except you skip the addresses and date at the top and begin directly with the salutation. You'll also need to pay particular attention to the subject line of your email. Be sure that it is specific to the position you are applying for.

In all cases, it's really important to follow the employer's instructions on how to submit your cover letter and résumé. Some employers direct you to a section on their website where you can upload your résumé. In these cases, it may not be obvious where your cover letter content should go. Look for a text box labeled something like "personal statement" or "additional information." Those are good places to add whatever you would normally write in a cover letter. If there doesn't seem to be anywhere like that, see if there is an email link to the hiring manager or whoever will be reading your résumé. Go ahead and send your "cover email" to this address, mentioning that you have uploaded your résumé (again omitting the addresses and date at the top of your cover letter). Try to use the person's name if it's been given.

LINKING-IN WITH IMPACT

As well as your paper or electronic résumé, creating a LinkedIn profile is a good way to highlight your experience and promote yourself, as well as to network. Joining professional organizations and connecting with other people in your desired field are good ways to keep abreast of changes and trends and work opportunities.

The key elements of a LinkedIn profile are your photo, your headline, and your profile summary. These are the most revealing parts of the profile and the ones employers and connections will base their impression of you on.

The photo should be carefully chosen. Remember that LinkedIn is not Facebook or Instagram: it is not the place to share a photo of you acting too casually on vacation or at a party. According to Joshua Waldman, author of *Job Searching with Social Media for Dummies*, the choice of photo should be taken seriously and be done right. These are his tips:

- Choose a photo in which you have a nice smile.
- Dress in professional clothing.
- Ensure the background of the photo is pleasing to the eye. According to Waldman, some colors—like green and blue—convey a feeling of trust and stability.
- Remember, it's not a mug shot. You can be creative with the angle of your photo rather than stare directly into the camera.
- Use your photo to convey some aspect of your personality.
- Focus on your face. Remember visitors to your profile will see only a small thumbnail image, so be sure your face takes up most of it.

Interviewing Skills

Sooner or later, your job search will result in what you've been hoping for (or, perhaps, dreading): a phone call or email requesting that you appear for an interview. When you get that call or email, it means they're interested in you and are considering hiring you.

Being prepared will help you feel less stressed during a job interview.
ANDREYPOPOV/ISTOCK/GETTY IMAGES

WHAT ARE EMPLOYERS LOOKING FOR?

When companies want to hire new employees, they list job descriptions on job hunting websites. These are a fantastic resource for you long before you're ready to actually apply for a job. You can read real job descriptions for real jobs and see what qualifications and experience are needed for the kinds of job that you're interested in. You can see what sort of tasks you'll be carrying out in different kinds of jobs. You'll also get a good idea of the range of salaries and benefits that go with different levels of experience.

Pay attention to the required qualifications, of course, but also pay attention to the desired qualifications: these are the ones you don't *have* to have, but if you have them, you'll have an edge over other potential applicants.

Here are a few to get you started:

www.monster.com   www.glassdoor.com
www.indeed.com   www.simplyhired.com
www.ziprecruiter.com

The best way to avoid nerves and keep calm when you're interviewing is to be prepared. It's okay to feel scared, but keep it in perspective. It's likely that you'll receive many more rejections in your professional life than acceptances, as we all do. However, you only need one "yes" to start out. Think of the interviewing process as a learning experience.

Personal contacts can make the difference! Don't be afraid to contact other professionals you know. Personal connections can be a great way to find jobs and internship opportunities. Your high school teachers, your coaches and mentors, and your friends' parents are all examples of people who very well may know about jobs or opportunities that would suit you. Start asking several months before you hope to start a job or internship, because it will take some time to do research and arrange interviews. You can also use social media in your search. LinkedIn, for example, includes lots of searchable information on local companies. Follow and interact with people on social media to get their attention. Just remember to act professionally and communicate with proper grammar, just as you would in person.

With the right attitude, you will learn from each experience and get better with each subsequent interview. That should be your overarching goal. Consider these tips and tricks when interviewing, whether it be for a job, internship, college admission, or something else entirely:

- Practice interviewing with a friend or relative. Practicing will help calm your nerves and make you feel more prepared. Ask for specific feedback from your friends. Do you need to speak louder? Are you making enough eye contact? Are you actively listening when the other person is speaking?
- Learn as much as you can about the company, school, or organization. Also be sure to understand the position for which you're applying. This will show the interviewer that you are motivated and interested in their organization.
- Speak up during the interview. Convey to the interviewer important points about you. Don't be afraid to ask questions. Try to remember the interviewers' names and call them by name.

- Arrive early and dress professionally and appropriately (you can read more about proper dress in a later section).
- Take some time to prepare answers to commonly asked questions. Be ready to describe your career or educational goals to the interviewer.

Common questions you may be asked during a job interview include these:

- Tell me about yourself.
- What are your greatest strengths?
- What are your weaknesses?
- Tell me something about yourself that's not on your résumé.
- What are your career goals?
- How do you handle failure? Are you willing to fail?
- How do you handle stress and pressure?
- What are you passionate about?
- Why do you want to work for us?

Tip: Bring a notebook and a pen to the interview. That way you can take some notes, and they'll give you something to do with your hands.

Common questions you may be asked during a college admissions interview include these:

- Tell me about yourself.
- Why are you interested in going to college?
- Why do you want to major in this subject?
- What are your academic strengths?
- What are your academic weaknesses? How have you addressed them?
- What will you contribute to this college/school/university?
- Where do you see yourself in ten years?
- How do you handle failure? Are you willing to fail?
- How do you handle stress and pressure?
- Whom do you most admire?
- What is your favorite book?

- What do you do for fun?
- Why are you interested in this college/school/university?

Jot down notes about your answers to these questions, but don't try to memorize the answers. You don't want to come off too rehearsed during the interview. Remember to be as specific and detailed as possible when answering these questions. Your goal is to set yourself apart in some way from the other people they will interview. Always accentuate the positive, even when you're asked about something you did not like, or about failure or stress. Most important, though, be yourself.

Active listening is the process of fully concentrating on what is being said, understanding it, and providing nonverbal cues and responses to the person talking. It's the opposite of being distracted and thinking about something else when someone is talking. Active listening takes practice. You might find that your mind wanders and you need to bring it back to the person talking (and this could happen multiple times during one conversation). Practice this technique in regular conversations with friends and relatives. In addition to helping you do better in an interview, it can cut down on nerves and make you more popular with friends and family, as everyone wants to feel that they are really being heard. (For more on active listening, check out https://www.mindtools.com/CommSkll/ActiveListening.htm.)

You should also be ready to ask questions of your interviewer. In a practical sense, there should be some questions that you have that you can't find the answer to on the website or in the literature. Also, asking questions shows that you are interested and have done your homework. Avoid asking questions about salary/scholarships or special benefits at this stage, and don't about anything negative that you've heard about the company or school. Keep the questions positive and relative to you and the position to which you're applying. Some example questions to potential employers include these:

- What is a typical career path for a person in this position?
- How would you describe the ideal candidate for this position?
- How is the department organized?

- What kinds of responsibilities come with this job? (Don't ask this if they've already addressed this question in the job description or discussion.)
- What can I do as a follow-up?
- When do you expect to reach a decision?

See the section in chapter 3 entitled "Make the Most of Campus Visits" for some good example questions to ask the college admissions office. The important thing is to write your own questions related to answers you really want to know. This will show genuine interest. Be sure your question isn't answered on the website, in the job description, or in the literature.

TO SHAKE OR NOT TO SHAKE

A handshake is a traditional form of greeting, especially in business. When you arrive for a job interview—or just meet someone new—a good firm handshake shows that you are a person to be taken seriously.

But shaking hands is not done in every culture, and even in North America, the norm of shaking hands has changed. During the COVID-19 crisis, people stopped shaking hands in order to avoid spreading germs. As things get back to normal, some people will want to resume shaking hands and some people won't.

When you arrive for a job interview, follow the lead of the person you're meeting with. A respectful head nod or elbow touch is just fine.

Shaking hands in the 21st century is something to think twice about . . .
PEOPLEIMAGES/ISTOCK/GETTY IMAGES

JULIA ARCIERO: PROFESSOR OF MATHEMATICS

Julia Arciero

COURTESY OF JULIA ARCIERO.

Julia Arciero received a bachelor of science degree in mathematics from the University of Michigan and a PhD in applied mathematics from the University of Arizona. Along the way, she also received a master's degree from the University of Arizona. She spent three years as a postdoctoral fellow at the University of Pittsburgh in the Department of Mathematics (Complex Biological Systems Group), where she was funded by an NSF Research Training Grant and worked on math biology research problems.

She became an assistant professor at IUPUI (Indiana University—Purdue University Indianapolis) in the fall of 2011. In 2017, she was tenured and promoted to associate professor, which is her current title. She is in her tenth year at IUPUI.

Can you explain how you became interested in math as a career path?

I always enjoyed math and science in school, and so upon entering college I knew that I wanted to major in mathematics in hopes of eventually teaching math at the high school or college level.

After my first two years following the typical mathematics undergraduate course sequence, a college adviser mentioned a summer research opportunity to me. I applied for this summer REU (research experience for undergraduates) program, which was NSF funded. I spent eight to ten weeks doing summer research with a math faculty mentor who was conducting mathematical biology/cancer research. Applying math to solve problems in biology was really exciting to me! I loved combining math and medicine/science. I worked for that professor for the next two years, until I graduated. Our research project involved developing a mathematical model of tumor and immune system dynamics. We explored the impact of immunotherapy on aggressive tumors.

During the REU, I learned not only about the research process but also about graduate school options. Participating in the REU was a turning point in my academic career because it helped me discover that I wanted to pursue a PhD in applied math. I applied to graduate schools all across the country and chose to attend the University of Arizona because they had an excellent applied math program that was strong in math biology research.

What's a "typical" day in your job?

As a tenured professor, I would say that about 30 percent of my job is teaching and 70 percent is doing research. I am at a research institution, so there is a strong research component. I teach two courses in the fall and two in the spring. I typically teach calculus, differential equations, 400-level math modeling classes, and some applied math graduate courses.

On my teaching days, I give my two lectures (which are seventy-five minutes each) and hold office hours where students can come ask questions, get help, and so on. I also have research meetings—I meet with students I am mentoring (PhD students) to monitor their progress on their research. I also have undergrad research students (usually in the summer) who I meet with weekly and give them new topics or questions to consider. I also have meetings with my research collaborators, such as other mathematicians, biologists, and medical professionals. In addition, I spend time writing papers and grants to fund our research.

There is also a service component to my position—usually in the form of serving on various committees in my department and school. I am on the advisory committee, I am chair of the awards committee, and I am the president of the steering committee.

Then there is the time I spend working on my research—this includes coding (typically in Matlab), designing components of the math model, analyzing the model computationally, and interpreting the model results.

How has the field of applied math changed since you have worked in it?

You can see how it's changing by what the NSF and the NIH are funding—right now it's big data, deep learning, and AI. There are a lot of grant proposal calls in those areas. Math biology continues to be a hot topic, and an interdisciplinary approach is highly desired now. You need experts from different fields to resolve complex problems. One scientist in a room alone won't solve COVID-19, for example. You have to be able to look at problems from all different aspects. There's a push toward interdisciplinary work and a greater focus on big data.

What's the best part of being in this field?

Well—I love my job. I feel very fortunate to have it. I would absolutely so this all again if I had the opportunity. For one, I really do love working with students! When you are in front of a class and learning together, it's special. Being with students makes me feel energized. Math is truly the language of all science! Mentoring students in research is also great—I learn from them. I love learning and have a deep love for education.

Also, I love that my position is flexible. I can make my own hours and can do my research work from anywhere. It's mobile and flexible. Aside from teaching and meetings, I can shift my schedule as needed.

I also love the research aspect. It's impactful, especially when you're dealing with medicine. Mathematics has such a large impact not just on science, but on everyday life. I wonder if people know that mathematicians are the ones that make it possible to do a Google search or look for items to buy on Amazon. That's exciting to me!

What's the most challenging part of this field?

Sometimes students are also the most challenging part, when they don't take responsibility for their education. Students should want to learn and understand, even when it's hard. It takes hours of practice and time to get good at anything. When my students don't meet me halfway, that is a challenge. I want my students to succeed and to know the material, but they have to come to class, meet with me, and do their homework for such success to happen!

Another challenge is when you get stuck working on your research. Sometimes you hit a roadblock—you've spent a long time trying to do something and then you can't go further. That can be challenging.

Do you think the current education adequately prepares students to enter the field?

Absolutely. If you take your math courses seriously, you'll be ready. The US education system promotes a well-rounded education that includes a wide variety of courses in addition to those in your major discipline. In other countries (such as in Asia and Europe), students take many more courses just in their discipline. Because of that, Americans typically do not score as well on assessments such as the Math Subject Test GRE, mainly because they have had less mathematics coursework than their international counterparts. That said, if you work hard and understand the material, you will have learned some serious mathematics and can apply it to any industry. Math teaches you how to think and reason and solve problems, which are skills needed across all disciplines and careers.

Where do you see the field going in the future?

There currently seems to be a big push toward AI. So many things are becoming automated these days. Certainly a lot of mathematics and statistics are involved in AI. Math as a whole will continue to be used and applied to all kinds of fields. Math is the language of all science! Pure math folks are proving mathematical principles that can then be used to solve problems in other disciplines like engineering, design, chemistry, biology, and physics. The future means uncovering the interdisciplinary connections of all these different fields.

What traits or skills make for a good mathematician?

You should be detail-oriented (you have to pay attention to all the details, because one thing can throw everything off and you'll get wrong results). You also need to be patient, because finding answers is hard work that requires many steps. You have to stay with problems for a while. You also should be able to generate questions of your own—be curious! Pay attention to what's going on in the world around you and why it's happening. Also, don't be afraid to work hard. There's a lot of perspiration as a mathematician!

What advice do you have for young people considering a career in math?

I believe that pursuing a degree in math is very smart choice—it prepares you for a great many things. You will get a deeper understanding of many things—the why, the how, and knowing how to ask questions. As an example, while I was an applied math graduate student, I had to take five graduate courses outside of math, but related to my area of application (biomedical engineering). At first, five classes at the graduate level in biomedical engineering sounded daunting. But I ended up doing the top work in those engineering classes, and I think it was because I had the foundation of math to help me answer the questions. Foundations in math help immensely!

You can do a lot with math. Studying math allows you to pursue any kind of science or even law school or medicine. You learn how to approach problems with reason and logic. You become curious. It puts you on a very strong footing for your career path, no matter what that path is. It teaches you how to think.

How can a young person prepare for this career while in high school?

Develop good learning techniques in high school. It's not about memorizing things. Ultimately, you need to *understand* these things. If you truly understand what is going on, then you'll remember it forever. Then try teaching the concepts to someone else. Explaining concepts to someone else is a great way to see if you really know the material.

Also, get to know someone in the field. Talking to people in the field will help you see what they really do and give you a better idea of whether you want to that for a living. Learn what people do with math degrees!

DRESSING APPROPRIATELY

It's important to determine what is actually appropriate in the setting of the interview. What is appropriate in a corporate setting might be different from what you'd expect as a small liberal arts college or at a large hospital setting. Most college admissions offices suggest "business casual" dress, for example, but depending on the job interview, you may want to step it up from there. Again, it's important to do your homework and come prepared. In addition to reading up on their guidelines, it never hurts to take a look around the site if you can to see what other people are wearing to work or to interviews. Regardless of the setting, make sure your clothes are not wrinkled, untidy, or stained. Avoid flashy clothing of any kind.

The term "business casual" means less formal than business attire like a suit, but a step up from jeans, T-shirt, and sneakers:

- *For men:* You can't go wrong with khaki pants, a polo or button-up shirt, and brown or black shoes.
- *For women:* Nice slacks, a shirt or blouse that isn't too revealing, and nice flats or shoes with a heel that's not too high.

Do the proper research to find out exactly how you should dress for your interview.
PEOPLEIMAGES/ISTOCK/GETTY IMAGES

FOLLOW-UP COMMUNICATION

Be sure to follow up, whether in email or via regular mail, with a thank-you note to the interviewer. This is true whether you're interviewing for a job or an internship, or interviewing with a college. A handwritten thank-you note, posted in the actual mail, is best. In addition to being considerate, it will trigger the interviewer's memory about you, and it shows that you have genuine interest in the position, company, or school. Be sure to follow the business-letter format and highlight the key points of your interview and experience at the company/university. Be prompt with your thank-you! Put it in the mail the day after your interview (or send that email the same day).

What Employers Expect

Regardless of the job, profession, or field, there are universal characteristics that all employers (and schools, for that matter) look for in potential employees. At this early stage in your professional life, you have an opportunity to recognize which of these foundational characteristics are your strengths (and therefore highlight them in an interview) and which are weaknesses (and therefore continue to work on them and build them up).

> *Tip:* Always aim to make your boss's job easier, not harder. Keeping this simple concept in mind can take you a very long way in the business world. By the same token, being able to convince an employer that you love to learn new things is one of the best ways to turn yourself into a candidate they won't be able to pass up.

Consider these universal characteristics that all employers look for:

- Positive attitude
- Dependability
- Desire to continue to learn
- Initiative
- Curiosity
- Effective communication
- Cooperation
- Organization

This is not an exhaustive list, and other characteristics can very well include things like being sensitive to others, being honest, having good judgment, being loyal, being responsible, and being on time. Specifically, in mathematics and statistics, you can add self-motivation, patience, perseverance, and attention to detail. Consider these important characteristics when you answer the common questions that employers ask. It pays to work these traits into the answers, of course being honest and realistic about yourself.

BEWARE WHAT YOU SHARE ON SOCIAL MEDIA

Most of us engage in social media. Sites such as Facebook, Twitter, Snapchat, TikTok, and Instagram provide us a platform for sharing photos and memories, opinions and life events, and reveal everything from our political stance to our sense of humor. It's a great way to connect with people around the world, but once you post something, it's accessible to anyone—including potential employers—unless you take mindful precautions.

Your posts may be public, which means you may be making the wrong impression without realizing it. More and more, people are using search engines like Google to get a sense of potential employers, colleagues, or employees, and the impression you make online can have a strong impact on how you are perceived. According to CareerBuilder.com, 60 percent of employers search for information on candidates on social media sites.

Glassdoor.com offers the following tips for how to avoid your social media activity from sabotaging your career success:

- Check your privacy settings. Ensure that your photos and posts are only accessible to the friends or contacts you want to see them. You want to come across as professional and reliable.
- Rather than avoid social media while searching for a job, use it to your advantage. Give future employees a sense of your professional interest by "liking" pages or joining groups of professional organizations related to your career goals.
- Grammar counts. Be attentive to the quality of writing of all your posts and comments.

- Be consistent. With each social media outlet, there is a different focus and tone of what you are communicating. LinkedIn is very professional while Facebook is far more social and relaxed. It's okay to take a different tone on various social media sites, but be sure you aren't blatantly contradicting yourself.
- Choose your username carefully. Remember, social media may be the first impression anyone has of you in the professional realm.

Effectively Handling Stress

As you're forging ahead with your life plans, whether it's college, a full-time job, or even a gap year, you might find that these decisions feel very important and heavy and that the stress is difficult to deal with. First off, that's completely normal. Try these simple stress-relieving techniques:

- Take deep breaths in and out. Try this for thirty seconds. You'll be amazed at how it can help.
- Close your eyes and clear your mind.
- Go scream at the passing subway car. Or lock yourself in a closet and scream. Or scream into a pillow. For some people, this can really help.
- Keep the issue in perspective. Any decision you make now can be changed if it doesn't work out.

Want ways to avoid stress altogether? They are surprisingly simple. Of course, simple doesn't always mean easy, but it means they are basic and make sense with what we know about the human body:

- Get enough sleep
- Eat healthy
- Get exercise
- Go outside
- Schedule downtime
- Connect with friends and family

The bottom line is that you need to take time for self-care. There will always be conflict, but how you deal with it makes all the difference. This only becomes increasingly important as you enter college or the workforce and maybe have a family. Developing good, consistent habits related to self-care now will serve you all your life!

Summary

Well, you made it to the end of this book! Hopefully, you have learned enough about mathematics and statistics to start along your journey, or to continue with your path. If you've reached the end and you feel like mathematics or statistics is your passion, that's great news. Or, if you've figured out that it isn't the right field for you, that's good information to learn, too. For many of us, figuring out what we *don't* want to do and what we *don't* like is an important step in finding the right career.

The best way to figure out what you want to do for a living is to get out there and start trying things!
BRIANAJACKSON/ISTOCK/GETTY IMAGES

There is a lot of good news about this field, and it's a very smart career choice for anyone with a passion for numbers. It's a great career for people who get energy from solving problems. Job demand is very strong. No matter which field you choose, demand is very high for this career! Having a plan and an idea about your future can help guide your decisions. We hope that by reading this book, you are well on your way to having a plan for your future. Good luck to you as you move ahead!

Glossary

accreditation: The act of officially recognizing an organizational body, person, or educational facility as having a particular status or being qualified to perform a particular activity. For example, schools and colleges are accredited. (See also *certification*.)

ACT: The American College Test (ACT) is one of the standardized college entrance tests that anyone wanting to enter undergraduate studies in the United States should take. It measures knowledge and skills in mathematics, English, reading, and science reasoning, as they apply to college readiness. There are four multiple-choice sections. There is also an optional writing test. The top score of the ACT is 36. (See also *SAT*.)

actuaries: These professionals analyze statistical data—such as mortality, accident, sickness, disability, and retirement rates—and create probability tables. The goal is to forecast risk and liability for payment of future benefits. They may also determine insurance rates and calculate cash reserves necessary to pay future benefits.

algorithm: The series of steps/formula/process that is followed to arrive at a result.

associate's degree: A degree awarded by community or junior colleges that typically requires two years of study.

bachelor's degree: An undergraduate degree awarded by colleges and universities that's typically a four-year course of study when pursued full-time. However, this can vary by degree earned and by the university awarding the degree.

certification: The action or process of confirming certain skills or knowledge on a person. Usually provided by some third-party review, assessment, or educational body. Individuals, not organizations, are certified. (See also *accreditation*.)

code: A set of instructions and commands read by a computer. Also called a programming language, code comes in many varieties for different uses, including assembly, compiled, interpreted, and object-oriented languages. (See also *programming language.*)

cybersecurity: A set of techniques put in place to protect the safety and integrity of networks and other Internet-connected systems from attacks. This includes securing their hardware, software, and data.

doctorate degree: The highest level of degree awarded by colleges and universities. Qualifies the holder to teach at the university level. Requires (usually published) research in the field. Typically requires an additional three to five years of study after earning a bachelor's degree. Anyone with a doctorate degree can be addressed as a "doctor," not just medical doctors.

economists: These professionals conduct research, prepare reports, or create plans to tackle economic problems related to the production and distribution of goods and services or monetary and fiscal policy. They may collect and process economic data using sampling techniques and methods.

gap year: A gap year is a year between high school and college (or sometimes between college and postgraduate studies) whereby the student is not in school but is instead typically involved in volunteer programs, such as the Peace Corps, in travel experiences, or in work and teaching experiences.

grants: Money to pay for postsecondary education that is typically awarded to students who have financial needs, but can also be used in the areas of athletics, academics, demographics, veteran support, and special talents. Grants do not have to be paid back.

master's degree: A secondary degree awarded by colleges and universities that requires at least one additional year of study after obtaining a bachelor's degree. The degree holder shows mastery of a specific field.

personal statement: A written description of your accomplishments, outlook, interest, goals, and personality that's an important part of your college application. The personal statement should set you apart from others. The required length depends on the institution, but they generally range from 1 to 2 pages, or 500–1,000 words.

postdoc: A postdoctoral researcher is a person who has completed their doctoral studies (usually their PhD) and is conducting research professionally. The goal of a postdoctoral research position is to pursue additional research or training in order to be able to pursue a career in academia, research, or any other fields.

postsecondary degree: Educational degree above and beyond a high school education. This is a general description that includes trade certificates and certifications, associate degrees, bachelor's degrees, master's degrees, and beyond.

programmer: A general term for a person (or machine) who writes code and creates and tests computer programs. Programmers usually specialize in one or a few programming languages. Areas of expertise include software development, database development, hardware programming, and web development.

research analysts: Operations research analysts create and apply mathematical models to develop and interpret information that helps management with decision making. Market research analysts research, analyze, interpret, and present data related to markets, operations, economics, customers, and other information related to the field they work in. For example, they may study market conditions to examine potential sales of a product or service.

SAT: The Scholastic Aptitude Test (SAT) is one of the standardized tests in the United States that anyone applying to undergraduate studies should take. It measures verbal and mathematical reasoning abilities as they relate to predicting successful performance in college. It is intended to complement a student's GPA and school record in assessing readiness for college. The total score of the SAT is 1600. (See also *ACT.*)

scholarships: Merit-based aid used to pay for postsecondary education that does not have to be paid back. Scholarships are typically awarded based on academic excellence or some other special talent, such as music or art.

statisticians: Professionals who develop or apply mathematical or statistical theory and methods to collect, organize, interpret, and summarize data. The goal is to provide usable information. They may specialize in fields such as biostatistics or agricultural, business, or economic statistics.

tenure: To give someone a permanent job, especially as a teacher or professor. A *tenured post* is an unlimited academic appointment that can be terminated only for cause or due to extraordinary circumstances, such as the program being discontinued. (See also *tenure-track faculty member.*)

tenure-track faculty member: The tenure track is a professor's path to promotion and academic job security. It's the process whereby an assistant professor becomes an associate professor and then a professor. Once you're a professor, you are *tenured.* An assistant professorship is the entry-level tenure-track position; lecturers and adjunct professors are not typically on the tenure rack. (See also *tenure.*)

Notes

Introduction

1. https://online.maryville.edu/blog/statistician-vs-mathematician/
2. https://www.businessinsider.com/high-paying-jobs-for-people-who-love-math-2016-6
3. https://www.bls.gov/ooh/math/mathematicians-and-statisticians.htm
4. Ibid.

Chapter 1

1. https://www.quora.com/What-is-the-difference-between-a-theoretical-statistician-and-an-applied-statistician-What-are-the-topics-a-theoretical-statistician-should-know-about
2. https://www.northeastern.edu/graduate/blog/what-do-statisticians-do/
3. Ibid.
4. https://policy.ku.edu/sites/policy.ku.edu/files/FEPMath_20170502.pdf
5. https://marktomforde.com/academic/undergraduates/WhatProfessorsDo.html
6. https://www.storyofmathematics.com/
7. https://marktomforde.com/academic/undergraduates/WhatProfessorsDo.html
8. https://www.salary.com/research/salary/benchmark/professor-mathematics-salary
9. https://www.bls.gov/ooh/math/actuaries.htm#tab-2
10. Ibid.
11. https://www.bls.gov/ooh/math/actuaries.htm
12. https://www.bls.gov/ooh/business-and-financial/market-research-analysts.htm

13. https://www.ziprecruiter.com/e/How-to-Become-an-Economic-Analyst

14. https://www.careerexplorer.com/careers/security-software-developer/

15. https://www.bls.gov/ooh/business-and-financial/market-research-analysts .htm#tab-2

16. https://www.bls.gov/ooh/life-physical-and-social-science/economists .htm#tab-3

17. http://www2.york.psu.edu/~dxl31/majweb.html

18. https://www.bls.gov/ooh/life-physical-and-social-science/economists .htm#tab-2

19. https://www.bls.gov/ooh/life-physical-and-social-science/economists.htm

20. https://drexel.edu/coas/academics/undergraduate-programs/mathematics/

21. https://www.bls.gov/ooh/math/mathematicians-and-statisticians.htm

22. https://www.bls.gov/news.release/pdf/ecopro.pdf

23. https://www.bls.gov/ooh/math/mathematicians-and-statisticians.htm

24. https://www.naceweb.org/uploadedfiles/files/2020/publication/executive -summary/2020-nace-salary-survey-winter-executive-summary.pdf

Chapter 2

1. https://onlinemathdegrees.org/who-hires-math-majors/

2. Lou Adler, "Survey Reveals 85% of All Jobs Are Filled via Networking," LinkedIn. com, February 29, 2016, https://www.linkedin.com/pulse/new-survey -reveals-85-all-jobs-filled-via-networking-lou-adler/.

Chapter 3

1. Gap Year Association, "Gap Year Data and Benefits," https://www.gapyearasso ciation.org/data-benefits.php

2. US News & World Report, "Finding a Good College Fit," https://www .usnews.com/education/blogs/the-college-admissions-insider/2011/06/13 /finding-a-good-college-fit

3. National Center for Education Statistics, "Fast Facts: Graduation Rates," n.d., https://nces.ed.gov/fastfacts/display.asp?id=40

4. US Department of Education, "Focusing Higher Education on Student Success," https://www.ed.gov/news/press-releases/fact-sheet-focusing-higher-education -student-success

5. Department of Education, National Center for Education Statistics. Digest for Education Statistics. https://nces.ed.gov/programs/digest/d14/tables /dt14_502.30.asp; Bureau of Labor Statistics. Current Population Survey. http://www.bls.gov/cps/cpsaat07.htm

6. https://nces.ed.gov/pubs2011/2011152.pdf

7. https://www.monster.com/career-advice/article/best-jobs-math-majors-0417

8. Allison Wignall. "Preference of the ACT or SAT by State (Infographic)." CollegeRaptor. https://www.collegeraptor.com/getting-in/articles/act-sat/pref erence-act-sat-state-infographic/ November 14, 2019

9. https://blog.prepscholar.com/which-schools-use-the-common-application -complete-list

10. BigFuture. "Focus on Net Price, Not Sticker Price." CollegeBoard. https://big future.collegeboard.org/pay-for-college/paying-your-share/focus-on-net-price -not-sticker-price

11. Jennifer Ma, Sandy Baum, Matea Pender, and C. J. Libassi. *Trends in College Pricing 2019* (New York: College Board, 2019). https://research.collegeboard.org/pdf /trends-college-pricing-2019-full-report.pdf

12. Ibid.

13. https://research.collegeboard.org/trends/college-pricing/figures-tables /average-net-price-sector-over-time

14. Federal Student Aid, An Office of the US Department of Education, "FAFSA Changes for 2017–2018," https://studentaid.ed.gov/sa/about/announce ments/fafsa-changes.

15. Edith Hamilton. Quoted in the *Saturday Evening Post*, September 27, 1958.

Chapter 4

1. Waldman, Joshua. *Job Searching with Social Media For Dummies*, 2nd ed. (Hoboken, NJ: John Wiley and Sons Publishing, 2013), p. 149.

2. Muchnick, Justin Ross. *Teens' Guide to College & Career Planning*, 12th ed. (Lawrenceville, NJ: Peterson's Publishing, 2015), pp. 179–80.

3. Mind Tools, "Active Listening: Hear What People Are Really Saying," https:// www.mindtools.com/CommSkll/ActiveListening.htm

4. CareerBuilder.com, press releases, http://www.careerbuilder.com/share/about us/pressreleasesdetail.aspx?ed=12%2F31%2F2016&id=pr945&sd =4%2F28%2F2016

5. Glassdoor.com, "9 Things to Avoid on Social Media While Looking for a New Job," https://www.glassdoor.com/blog/things-to-avoid-on-social-media-job-search/

Resources

*A*re you looking for more information about the professions in math/stats, or even want to learn more about a particular area of it? Do you want to know more about the college application process or need some help finding the right educational fit for you? Do you want a quick way to search for a good college or school? Try these resources as a starting point on your journey toward finding a fulfilling career in mathematics/statistics!

Books

Bolles, Richard N. *What Color Is Your Parachute? 2019: A Practical Manual for Job Hunters and Career Changers.* New York, NY: Ten Speed Press, revised edition, 2019.

Fiske, Edward. *Fiske Guide to Colleges.* Naperville, IL: Sourcebooks, Inc., 2018.

Hahn, Gerald J., and Necip Doganaksoy, *A Career in Statistics: Beyond the Numbers.* Hoboken, NJ: Wiley & Sons Publishing, 2011.

Hynson, Colin. *Dream Jobs in Math 2nd ed.* St. Catharines, ON, Canada: Crabtree Publishing Company, 2017.

Muchnick, Justin Ross. *Teens' Guide to College & Career Planning*, 12th ed. Lawrenceville, NJ: Peterson's Publishing, 2015.

Princeton Review. *The Best 382 Colleges, 2018 Edition: Everything You Need to Make the Right College Choice.* New York, NY: The Princeton Review, 2018.

Websites/Blogs

American Gap Year Association
gapyearassociation.org
The American Gap Year Association's mission is "making transformative gap years an accessible option for all high school graduates." A gap year is a year

taken between high school and college to travel, teach, work, volunteer, generally mature, and otherwise experience the world. Their website has lots of advice and resources for anyone considering taking a gap year.

American Mathematical Society
www.ams.org
The American Mathematical Society has been in existence since 1888. They advance research and connect the diverse global mathematical community through publications, meetings and conferences, MathSciNet, professional services, advocacy, and awareness programs. There are approximately 30,000 individuals and 570 institutions worldwide in the AMS.

Association for Women in Mathematics
awm-math.org
The Association for Women in Mathematics (AWM) is a nonprofit organization founded in 1971. It currently has more than 3,500 members representing a broad spectrum of the mathematical community, from the United States and around the world. The AWM has played a crucial role in increasing the presence and visibility of women in the mathematical sciences in its nearly fifty-year history.

The Balance Website
www.thebalance.com
This site is all about managing money and finances, but also has a large section called Your Career, which provides advice for writing résumés and cover letters, interviewing, and more. Search the site for teens and you can find teen-specific advice and tips.

Codecademy
www.codecademy.com
This website is an effective and easy way to learn to code. It includes short modules on HTML, CSS, and website development, after which you can move on to other programming languages. The courses are easy to follow, and they award badges when you finish each one, which can be a nice motivator to keep learning.

College Entrance Examination Board Website
www.collegeboard.org
The College Entrance Examination Board tracks and summarizes financial
data from colleges and universities all over the United States. This site can be
your one-stop shop for all things college research. It contains lots of advice and
information about taking and doing well on the SAT and ACT tests, many
articles on college planning, a robust college searching feature, a scholarship
searching feature, and a major and career search area. You can type your career
of interest (for example, statistics) into the search box and get back a full page
that describes the career, gives advice on how to prepare, where to get experience, how to pay for it, what characteristics you should have to excel in this
career, lists of helpful classes to take while in high school, and lots of links for
more information. A great, well-organized site.

College Grad Career Profile Website
www.collegegrad.com/careers
Although this site is primarily geared toward college graduates, the careers profile area, indicated above, has a list of links to nearly every career you could
ever think of. A single click takes you to a very detailed, helpful section that
describes the job in detail, explains the educational requirements, includes links
to good colleges that offer this career, includes links to actual open jobs and
internships, describes the licensing requirements, if any, lists salaries, and much
more.

GoCollege
www.gocollege.com
GoCollege.com calls itself the number one college-bound website on the
Internet. It includes lots of good tips and information about getting money
and scholarships for college and getting the most out of your college education.
Has a good section on how scholarships, in general, work.

Go Overseas
www.gooverseas.com
Go Overseas claims to be your guide to more than 14,000 study and teach
abroad programs that will change how you see the world. Also includes information about high school abroad programs, and gap year opportunities. It

includes community reviews and information about finding programs specific to your interests and grade-level teaching aspirations.

Khan Academy
www.khanacademy.org
The Khan Academy website is an impressive collection of articles, courses, and videos about many educational topics in math, science, and the humanities. You can search any topic or subject (by subject matter and grade), and read lessons, take courses, and watch videos to learn all about it. Includes test prep information for the SAT, ACT, AP, GMAT, and other standardized tests. There is also a College Admissions tab with lots of good articles and information, provided in the approachable Khan style.

Live Career Website
www.livecareer.com
This site has an impressive number of resources directed toward teens for writing résumés and cover letters, and interviewing.

Mapping Your Future
www.mappingyourfuture.org
This site helps young people figure out what they want to do and maps out how to reach career goals. Includes helpful tips on résumé writing, job hunting, job interviewing, and more.

The Mathematical Association of America
www.maa.org
The Mathematical Association of America is the world's largest community of mathematicians, students, and enthusiasts. Their mission is to advance the understanding of mathematics and its impact on the world. Members include university, college, and high school teachers; graduate and undergraduate students; pure and applied mathematicians; computer scientists; statisticians; STEM professionals, and many others in academia, government, business, and industry.

Monster

www.monster.com

Monster.com is perhaps the most well-known, and certainly one of the largest, employment websites in the United States. You fill in a couple of search boxes and away you go. You can sort by job title, of course, as well as by company name, location, salary range, experience range, and much more. The site also includes information about career fairs, advice on résumés and interviewing, and more.

Occupational Outlook Handbook

www.bls.gov

The US Bureau of Labor Statistics produces this website. It offers lots of relevant and updated information about various careers, including average salaries, how to work in the industry, the job's outlook in the job market, typical work environments, and what workers do on the job. (See www.bls.gov/emp/ for a full list of employment projections.)

Peterson's College Prep Website

www.petersons.com

In addition to lots of information about preparing for the ACT and SAT tests and easily searchable information about scholarships nationwide, Peterson's website includes a comprehensive searching feature to search for universities and schools based on location, major, name, and more.

Princeton Review Website

www.princetonreview.com/quiz/career-quiz

This site includes a very good aptitude test geared toward high schoolers to help them determine their interests and find professions that complement those interests.

Society of Industrial and Applied Mathematics

www.siam.org

The Society of Industrial and Applied Mathematics (SIAM) is an international community of over 14,000 members. Nearly 500 academic, manufacturing, research and development, service and consulting organizations, government, and military organizations worldwide are institutional members. It was incorporated in 1952 as a nonprofit organization to convey useful mathematical knowledge to other professionals who could implement mathematical theory for practical, industrial, or scientific use.

Study.Com Website
www.study.com
A site similar to Khan Academy, where you can search any topic or subject and read lessons, take courses, and watch videos to learn all about it.

TeenLife: College Preparation
www.teenlife.com
This organization calls itself "the leading source for college preparation" and it includes lots of information about summer programs, gap year programs, community service, and more. They believe that spending time out "in the world" outside of the classroom can help students develop important life skills. This site contains lots of links to volunteer and summer programs.

US News & World Report College Rankings
www.usnews.com/best-colleges
US News & World Report provides almost fifty different types of numerical rankings and lists of colleges throughout the United States to help students with their college search. You can search colleges by best reviewed, best value for the money, best liberal arts schools, best schools for B students, and more.

PODCASTS

Data Skeptic
A detailed, yet extremely approachable, podcast about data science, artificial intelligence, and machine learning.

Freakonomics Radio
This podcast is from Stitcher and Stephen J. Dubner, coauthor of the *Freakonomics* books. Tells you things you always thought you knew (but didn't)

and things you never thought you wanted to know (but do)—from the economics of sleep to how to become great at just about anything.

Greater Than Code
For a long time, tech culture has focused too narrowly on technical skills; this has resulted in a tech community that too often puts companies and code over people. *Greater Than Code* is a podcast that invites the voices of people who are not heard from enough in tech—women, people of color, trans and/or queer folks—to talk about the human side of software development and technology.

Hidden Brain
A podcast by NPR, it calls itself "a conversation about life's unseen patterns." It helps curious people understand the world and themselves. Using science and storytelling, *Hidden Brain*'s host, Shankar Vedantam reveals the unconscious patterns that drive human behavior, the biases that shape our choices, and the triggers that direct our relationships.

How I Built This, with Guy Raz
In this NPR app, Guy Raz dives into the stories behind some of the world's best known companies. *How I Built This* weaves a narrative journey about innovators, entrepreneurs and idealists—and the movements they built.

Mathematical Moments from the AMS
This AMS (American Mathematical Society) podcast promotes appreciation and understanding of the role mathematics plays in science, nature, technology, and human culture. Listen to researchers talk about how they use math: from presenting realistic animation to beating cancer.

Women in Math: The Limit Does Not Exist
This podcast is an effort to promote visibility of women in mathematics. Inspired by the fact that women are vast minority in higher mathematics, it serves to increase enrollment and participation of women in mathematics and STEM courses.

Bibliography

Balance.com. "Career Choices," April 24, 2018. Retrieved October 3, 2020, from https://www.thebalance.com/career-choice-or-change-4161891.

Bureau of Labor Statistics, US Department of Labor, Healthcare Occupations website, www.bls.gov/ooh/healthcare. Various tabs.

CareerExplorer.com. "What Does a Biostatistician Do?" Retrieved September 10, 2020, from https://www.careerexplorer.com/careers/ biostatistician

CareerExplorer.com. "What Does a Mathematician Do?" Retrieved September 10, 2020, from https://www.careerexplorer.com/careers/ mathematician

College Entrance Examination Board. Retrieved October 3, 2020, from https:// bigfuture.collegeboard.org/pay-for-college/college-costs/understanding -college-costs.

Common Core State Standards Initiative. "Preparing American's Students for Success." Retrieved September 28, 2020, from http://www.corestandards .org.

Drexel University. "Bachelor's Degrees in Mathematics." Retrieved September 10, 2020, from https://drexel.edu/coas/academics/undergraduate-pro grams/mathematics/

Federal Student Aid, An Office of the U.S. Department of Education. "FAFSA Changes for 2017–2018." Retrieved September 15, 2020, from https:// studentaid.ed.gov/sa/about/announcements/fafsa-changes.

Fiske, Edward. *Fiske Guide to Colleges.* Naperville, IL: Sourcebooks, Inc., 2018.

Forbes.com. "12 Qualities Employers Look For When They're Hiring." Retrieved October 7, 2020, from https://www.forbes.com/sites/lizryan/2016 /03/02/12-qualities-employers-look-for-when-theyre-hiring/#8ba06d22 c242.

Gap Year Association. "Research Statement." Retrieved September 30, 2020, from https://gapyearassociation.org/research.php.

Glassdoor.com. "9 Things to Avoid on Social Media While Looking for a New Job." Retrieved September 18, 2020, from https://www.glassdoor.com /blog/things-to-avoid-on-social-media-job-search/

Go College, "Types of Scholarships." Retrieved September 30, 2020, from http://www.gocollege.com/financial-aid/scholarships/types/.

Keates, Cathy. "What Is Job Shadowing?" *TalentEgg*. Retrieved September 18, 2020, from https://talentegg.ca/incubator/2011/02/03/what-is-job -shadowing/.

The Ladders. "Keeping an Eye on Recruiter Behavior." Retrieved October 10, 2020, from https://cdn.theladders.net/static/images/basicSite/pdfs/TheLadders -EyeTracking-StudyC2.pdf.

LinkedIn.com, "New Survey Reveals 85% of All Jobs are Filled Via Networking." Retrieved October 10, 2020, from https://www.linkedin.com/pulse /new-survey-reveals-85-all-jobs-filled-via-networking-lou-adler/.

Ma, Jennifer, Sandy Baum, Matea Pender, and C. J. Libassi. *Trends in College Pricing 2019.* New York: College Board, 2019. Retrieved October 1, 2020, from https://research.collegeboard.org/pdf/trends-college-pricing-2019-full -report.pdf

Mind Tools. "Active Listening: Hear What People Are Really Saying." Retrieved October 10, 2020, from https://www.mindtools.com/CommSkll/Active Listening.htm.

Muchnick, Justin Ross. *Teens' Guide to College & Career Planning*, 12th ed. Lawrenceville, NJ: Peterson's Publishing, 2015, pp. 179–80.

National Center for Education Statistics. "Fast Facts: Graduation Rates." Retrieved October 10, 2020, from https://nces.ed.gov/fastfacts/display.asp ?id=40.

National Center for Education Statistics. "Private School Enrollment." Retrieved September 22, 2020, from https://nces.ed.gov/programs/coe /indicator_cgc.asp.

Northeastern University Graduate Programs. "What Do Statisticians Do? Roles, Responsibilities, and Career Paths." Retrieved September 30, 2020, from https://www.northeastern.edu/graduate/blog/what-do-statisticians-do/.

Online Math Degrees. "Who Hires Math Majors?" Retrieved September 20, 2020, from https://onlinemathdegrees.org/who-hires-math-majors/.

StoryofMathematics.com. "The Story of Mathematics." Retrieved September 5, 2020, from https://www.storyofmathematics.com/.

US Department of Education. "Focusing Higher Education on Student Success." Retrieved September 30, 2020, from https://www.ed.gov/news /press-releases/fact-sheet-focusing-higher-education-student-success.

US News & World Report. "Finding a Good College Fit." Retrieved September 18, 2020, from https://www.usnews.com/education/blogs/the-college -admissions-insider/2011/06/13/finding-a-good-college-fit.

Waldman, Joshua. *Job Searching with Social Media For Dummies,* 2nd ed. Hoboken, NJ: John Wiley and Sons Publishing, 2013, p. 149.

Wignall, Allison. "Preference of the ACT or SAT by State (Infographic)." CollegeRaptor. Retrieved October 1, 2020, from https://www.collegeraptor .com/getting-in/articles/act-sat/preference-act-sat-state-infographic/ November 14, 2019

ZipRecruiter.com. "How to Become an Economic Analyst." Retrieved September 10, 2020, from "https://www.ziprecruiter.com/e/How-to-Become-an -Economic-Analyst

About the Author

Kezia Endsley is an editor and author from Indianapolis, Indiana. In addition to editing technical publications and writing books for teens, she enjoys running and competing in triathlons, traveling, reading, and spending time with her family and many pets.